What's in a Word?

WHAT'S IN A WORD?

40 WORDS OF JESUS FOR THE 40 DAYS OF LENT

David Winter

 The Bible Reading Fellowship

Text copyright © David Winter 1994

Published by
The Bible Reading Fellowship
Peter's Way
Sandy Lane West
Oxford
OX4 5HG
ISBN 0 7459 2989 3
Albatross Books Pty Ltd
PO Box 320
Sutherland
NSW 2232
Australia
ISBN 0 7324 0913 6

First edition 1994

Acknowledgments
Unless otherwise stated, all Scripture quotations are
taken from the Holy Bible, New International Version.
Copyright © 1973, 1978, 1984 by International Bible Society.
Used by permission of Hodder & Stoughton Ltd. All rights
reserved.

A catalogue record for this book is available
from the British Library

Printed and bound in Great Britain
by Biddles Limited, Guildford

Contents

Introduction

What's in a word? One answer, I suppose, is as much as you can get out of it. In an underground train from Hong Kong to Kowloon I was wedged in with hundreds of Chinese commuters. The air was full of the music of their language. It was strangely pleasing, a bit like the sound of an aeolian harp—full of rising and falling tones, with a bell-like resonance. It sounded lovely, but I couldn't understand a word. It was speech, but it communicated nothing to me.

I suspect that Bible reading is sometimes like that. We hear its sounds, sometimes familiar, sometimes strange. We know that it's speech and we sense that it's important and deserves respect. But we simply can't understand it. It has words. But they do not say anything particular to us.

And we know it's not the Bible's fault, any more than it was the fault of those home-going Chinese that their words meant nothing to me. We have been taught, and most of us accept, that the Bible is the 'word' of God. As he is not one to play tricks on people, we may assume that his words not only have meaning, but should mean something to us. But they come at us in such an overwhelming way that we feel we simply can't cope with them.

I placed my plastic cup in one of those coffee-making machines, read the instructions and inserted my money. As though at a hidden signal, coffee flowed ... and flowed ... and flowed. Truly 'my cup runneth over'. So did the safety tray, the stand and eventually the carpet. I realized that having too much too soon is as unhelpful as having too little too late.

Sometimes it does seem to us that the Bible is coming to us in super-abundance. As the words pour over us, we may well feel swamped. Worse, when it comes to the season of Lent, we're told we ought to make room for more Bible study. Apparently, we're not doing enough! Our reaction may well be to walk away from it altogether. After all, if we find it difficult to cope with what we get now, how will we be able to make sense of even more?

This book offers a quite radical solution. Read less. In fact, for each of the next forty days, let just one word from the Bible—a word of Jesus—speak to you. The Sundays in Lent are not traditionally counted among the forty days, and for each of these there is one of the 'I am' sayings of Jesus from St John's Gospel to consider. As St Paul advised the Christians at Colosse, 'Let the word of Christ dwell in you richly.' For once, tighten the focus. Put a microscope to the Bible rather than a telescope and discover, very literally, 'what's in a word'.

Of course, we shall look at the word in its context and try to understand its particular significance and meaning. But it is only one word, and the book will have done its work if it makes just that one 'word of the Lord' come alive for you in a new way.

Seek

Jesus turned, and saw them following, and said to them, 'What do you seek?'

John 1:38 (RSV)

Children used to play a game called 'hide and seek'. Possibly they still do, though probably with a computer. Somebody hides and somebody else looks for them. Eventually the seeker either gives up or discovers the hiding place. It's as simple as that.

'Seek' is a word Jesus used quite often. Most people know that he said, 'Seek and you will find.' But in fact 'seek' is a common word all through the Bible and long before the coming of Jesus. 'When you seek me with all your heart,' said the prophet Jeremiah, 'you will find me.' The discovery of God—who he is, what he wishes, how he can help us—is a reward for those who seek him. The process of faith, in other words, is a journey of discovery. Like the children in the game, we seek and eventually we either give up or we discover ... well, whatever it was that was hidden from us. But unlike the hidden child, desperate not to be found, God has promised that those who truly seek him will find him. In other words, he actually wants to be found.

The particular 'word' of Jesus that I have chosen to start this journey of exploration is in the first chapter of John's Gospel. After the baptism of Jesus, and before he had begun to gather his twelve disciples, two of John the Baptist's disciples set out one day to follow him—literally. They walked behind him along the road, presumably to find out where he was going and what he was doing. Jesus turned round and saw them following. 'What do you seek?' he asked.

It was a simple phrase as he spoke it, and it has been translated just as 'What do you want?' But more accurately it was 'What are you looking for?' I prefer 'What do you seek?' because it conveys the seriousness and depth both of his question and of their search. They weren't just curious or being nosey. They were seeking something, and they were deadly serious about it. Jesus recognized and respected that seriousness. Until now they had thought that John the Baptist might be the one they were searching for, but he had recently pointed them away from himself to Jesus. 'I'm not fit to do up his shoe-laces,' he had told them. 'He is the Lamb of God, who takes away the sin of the world.'

Perhaps it was those words that prompted them that day to follow Jesus and find out if he was in fact the one they were seeking. At any rate, Jesus challenged their search: 'What are you looking for? What are you seeking?' It's more than 'wanting', because sometimes we can't possibly know what we want until we have set out on the search. It's as we look that we discover the possibilities.

Any spiritual journey worth the effort must begin with our answer to this disarmingly simple question of Jesus: 'What are you looking for?' In the rush of life and in the strait-jacket of routine we may have little time or space even to discover whether we are seeking anything. But at times most of us know that feeling of unease. There must be something more.

One August I approached a young couple who had turned up at our church in London. I'd never seen them before, and a few questions established that they weren't visitors, or refugees from another church, but local people making their first visit. I asked them why they'd come. They laughed, and said that on the previous Friday evening they'd both come home from work shattered, ate their pre-packed meal from the microwave and then slumped in front of the television until bed time. As they switched off the set, one of them remarked, 'There must be more to life than this.'

The comment set them talking into the night. Perhaps God had something to do with it? Neither was at all 'religious' and they weren't even occasional church-goers, but they decided there and then to go to the nearest church the next Sunday. And here they were!

And yes, the story does have a happy ending. Once they began to discover what they were looking for, they were on the way to wanting it and when they really wanted it they were most of the way to finding it. Many questions and much 'seeking' later, they were baptized and confirmed. What they were looking for was meaning and purpose in their lives. What they wanted was to discover a greater truth than 'ordinary' life and experience had brought them. And what they discovered was God himself.

What do you seek? What are you looking for? There are many people who already believe in God (like Andrew and John) but who still seek for deeper meaning and purpose, who still want to discover a greater truth than ordinary life and experience have brought them.

And as they seek, they can encourage themselves with this thought. The 'answer' is at the same time seeking them. Because Jesus said of himself that 'the Son of Man comes to seek and to save what was lost'.

A reflection

We can't know what it is we want until we discover what it is we are looking for.

A prayer

Lord, help me to turn my vague wants into a genuine search for truth. Amen.

For discussion

What do you think people in our modern society are really looking for? And how do they pursue their search for it?

Want

'What do you want me to do for you?' Jesus asked him.

Mark 10:51

If you conducted a poll among parents to discover which was the very first phrase or sentence that their children uttered, I suspect that high on the list would be 'I want' (or perhaps, less grammatically but even more forcefully, 'Me want'). One of our children went straight from incomprehensible baby-talk to clear-cut English in one never-to-be-forgotten sentence, 'I want Mummy.'

In other words, from a very early age we know what we want—or we think we do. And we know that in a competitive and selfish world we've got to get our bids in early. 'Want' is not the same as 'seek', because our wants can be very unfocused and vague, whereas what we seek is a priority, a clear and defined objective. But when we know what we are looking for, then that very search becomes a wanting. Once I have identified Mummy, I can want her. Once I have discovered ice cream, I can want some more.

So while 'seeking' is the first step in the journey of Christian discovery, 'wanting' follows on its heels. Allowing our wants to be shaped by a higher goal (what we are seeking) doesn't lessen our wants. Indeed, it may sharpen them.

In two consecutive stories in Mark's Gospel, Jesus asks an identical question. 'What do you want me to do for you?' The questions are word-for-word identical, but the circumstances are very different.

In the first instance, the disciples James and John approached Jesus with a very strange request. 'Teacher, we want you to do for us whatever we ask'. The reply of Jesus was that simple question, 'What do you want me to do for you?'

Their answer was audacious. 'Let one of us sit at your right and the other at your left in your glory.' In other words, please can we reserve in advance the best seats and the most influential places when the day of triumph dawns? As a request, it was pure 'want', unshaped by serious seeking. They simply didn't know what they were asking.

Jesus let them down gently. The seats at his right and left were already allocated. His 'glorification' was to happen shortly and it would involve drinking a bitter cup and being immersed in bitter suffering. They were, of course, very welcome to share that, but the prized positions couldn't be theirs—in fact, as we know, they were reserved for two thieves. Jesus was, in his own language, 'glorified' on the cross, and to share his glory was to take up his cross and surrender life in self-sacrificing love. That wasn't, clearly, what they had had in mind, though James himself did walk the path of martyrdom and John the path of exile. But at this moment they didn't know what they were asking. They wanted the glory, but not at the price of pain. They wanted to follow Jesus all the way to the kingdom, but not by way of the cross. Their wanting, in other words, was dominated by self-interest and was essentially superficial.

In the second story, Jesus was leaving Jericho, together with a large crowd. A blind beggar, Bartimaeus, was sitting by the roadside. 'When he heard that it was Jesus of Nazareth, he began to shout, "Jesus, Son of David, have mercy on me."' Although the bystanders told him to be quiet, Jesus heard him and called him over.

'What do you want me to do for you?' he asked him—exactly as he had asked James and John. The reply of Bartimaeus was as precise as theirs, and even shorter. 'Rabbi, I want to see.'

Bartimaeus knew what he was looking for, what he was seeking: his sight. To see would transform his whole life. But more than that, he knew that Jesus alone could help him. The rabbi who was the 'Son of David' could do for him what no one else could do. The opportunity was momentary—in a minute or two Jesus would be out of earshot, perhaps for ever. His life's search was focused in that single moment of time. It was literally now or never.

It is human to want 'things': position, power, influence, rank, possessions. But to make them the goal of our life's search is to be doomed to disappointment. James and John had to learn, and presumably did, that what they wanted was not necessarily the will of God for them and would not necessarily bring them the happiness and fulfilment for which they searched.

Bartimaeus, from his beggar's patch at the side of the road, had a clearer vision of what he was looking for, even though he was blind. Other things could and would follow—work, reputation, dignity, self-esteem—but it would all only begin to happen when the Son of David had mercy on him. His whole life's search at that moment was properly and adequately summed up in the simple request, 'I want to see.'

Our problem very often is that, like children, we don't know what we want. We know we want something. We sense gaps and an emptiness at the heart of life but we can't put that sense of wanting into words. James and John got it wrong. Bartimaeus got it right. Not because the former were selfish and the second was not— both requests were, in one sense, completely self-centred. But Bartimaeus threw himself on the Lord's mercy, and asked for no more than the absolute and fundamental necessity: 'I want to see.' And he knew that the only one who could actually meet his need was the one who was just for a minute or two within earshot.

'Jesus, Son of David, have mercy on me ... Rabbi, I want to see.'

Jesus said, 'What do you want me to do for you?' If he were saying that to you now, how would you reply? Like James and John, with a request for honour, privilege and power—even if it is in the religious realm? Or like Bartimaeus, with a humble request for new vision?

A reflection

Nobody fills a cup unless they know it's empty. Recognizing our emptiness is an essential first step to being 'filled'.

A prayer

Lord Jesus, like Bartimaeus I want to see. Open my inward eyes so that I can recognize both what I need and what you are willing to give me. Amen.

For discussion

The credit card slogan offered to 'take the waiting out of wanting'. Are there similar simplistic slogans in the spiritual realm?

Ask

'Ask and it will be given to you.'

Matthew 7:7

It's hard to think of any action more fundamental than asking. When the cat is making a thorough nuisance of herself, wrapping herself round my legs or scratching at the chair, I know that she is asking for something—usually for food. Children who can't yet frame the words can ask very eloquently for a drink or a biscuit. And I'm told by dog owners that their pets are able to communicate in an almost irresistible way that they would like to go for a walk.

And once we learn to speak, the possibilities are endless! All day long we are asking, in one way or another—for tickets, for information, for goods, for explanations. It's just as well someone invented the question mark.

So it's not surprising that we ask God questions, too. We ask him for things. We 'make our requests known to him', as St Paul puts it. And when we do that, we are simply doing what Jesus told us to do: 'Ask...'

But why do we need to? After all, God knows everything. The Bible tells us that he knows our thoughts before we think them and our requests before we make them (Psalm 139:3–4). So why do have to put them into words? Or, to put it another way, why does God make asking a condition of receiving? 'Ask and it will be given to you.' The clear implication is that if we do not ask we will not receive. Indeed, St James says as much: 'You do not have, because you do not ask God.' Why is 'asking' such an important element of our relationship with God?

The answer seems to lie in our own experience. As babies and then as children we learn to ask our parents for things, and in the process also learn what it is to trust. As adults, too, we know that good, loving relationships involve dependence—that mutual reliance on another to provide what we can't possibly provide for ourselves. It is certainly 'more blessed to give than to receive', but to receive is a blessing, because it puts us in a dependent role where someone else is concerned. I can ask something of someone who loves me and cares for me. Outside of a loving relationship, I must pay for what I want. Within it, I can ask and receive it as a gift, and, more than that, as a token or symbol of love.

The Greek word used here for 'ask' is one that implies that kind of dependence. It is always used when the one doing the asking is in a less powerful position than the one to whom the request is made—whether it is a human being to God, or a child to a parent, or a subject to a king, or even a beggar to a passer-by. We ask because we recognize that we are dependent. But when we ask God, we also know—as Jesus goes on to say in the Sermon on the Mount—that we are like children asking a favour of a father who loves us and wants the best for us. We are pushing on an open door.

Ask. It sounds so simple. Yet for many of us it is the real sticking point in our Christian journey. We don't want to feel that we can't cope, can't do it ourselves, need help even with the smallest concerns of the day, let alone the great problems of life. Stubbornly we refuse to ask, and as a consequence, 'it' is not given to us. And the 'it'—as Jesus explains—is the 'good gift' that God has for us, the best for his child that our simple request will release into our lives.

A reflection

The very act of asking is an act of humility.

SATURDAY
Find

'Does he not ... go after the lost sheep until he finds it?'

Luke 15:4

'Find' is a word that conveys a simple idea. We lose something ... and then we 'find' it again. That's its literal meaning, and it's something a child can easily understand. But we also use it metaphorically, when we 'find out' something. By enquiry or discovery we 'find' the truth. Something that was hidden to us before (how to program a video timer, perhaps), becomes part of our knowledge. 'I've found out how to do it,' we say triumphantly.

The Bible speaks of human beings seeking and wanting and asking to know the truth about God. St Paul told some Greek philosophers that God created us for the express purpose that we should 'seek him and perhaps reach out to him and find him'. Some years ago there was a very distinguished television series called 'The Long Search'. It was all about the human search for God. As the camera and microphone visited different cultures, races and religions, it unfolded a picture of people on an endless quest for the truth, which they saw as a search for God. Some felt that they had found him. More, it seemed to me, would only claim that they were still looking.

'If you seek me with all your heart,' God told his people in the Old Testament, 'you will find me.' He isn't a God who plays hide-and-seek with his creatures. He actually wants us to find him and know him and enjoy him for ever. As the writer of the letter to the

Hebrews put it, 'He rewards those who earnestly seek him.' Or, in the crisper words of Jesus, 'Those who seek, find.'

So the human search for God is not a hunt for the obscure. We are not chasing some will o' the wisp, an elusive hidden spirit. God wants us to seek, as we have seen, but he also wants us to find. That is why he has filled the universe with clues—the beauty and order of creation, the voice of conscience, the testimony of holy men and women . . . and above all the witness of Jesus, who could say to his followers, 'If you have seen me, you have seen the Father.'

But today's verse doesn't speak of our finding God, however important that is, but of God finding us. The most remarkable truth of the Christian faith, and the thing that distinguishes it from every other religion in the world, is that God comes to find us. He isn't content to watch his creatures searching here and there for clues about his nature or evidence of his love. He comes to us, he shows us himself, he stands beside us. That is what the incarnation is all about: God revealing what he is like in the person of his Son.

Jesus summed up his whole mission in that one memorable sentence: 'The Son of Man has come to seek and to save what was lost' (Luke 19:10). God took the initiative. It is important that we should look for him, seeking to find him in all his ways. It is even more important, and far more wonderful, that he is looking for us . . . and that he will not give up the search 'until he finds' what was lost.

A reflection

To engage in a serious search is in itself quite satisfying. But to find what we are searching for is still the object of the exercise.

A prayer

Heavenly Father, you have promised that those who seek you with all their hearts will find you. Help me to seek you, and also to realize when and where I have found you. Amen.

For discussion

Think of an explorer who has found a hitherto unknown valley, or a botanist who has found a new kind of shrub, or a researcher who has found a cure for a disease. Try to share their excitement. What should they then do with their discovery?

The light of the world

Jesus said ... 'I am the light of the world.'

John 8:12

Seven times in the Fourth Gospel Jesus says, 'I am', and these sayings have provided the Church ever since with seven profound pictures of his character. Because they are so well known, we may feel that they have lost their ability to surprise us, but in a book about the 'words' of Jesus we can hardly ignore them. They are Christ's 'charter', a summary of his role in the purpose of the Father.

And this first saying picks up a theme that runs right through John's Gospel—the theme of life. The world was in darkness: the darkness of separation from God. But the world in its rejection of God was not rejected by God. He loved the 'world', even the world that had 'loved darkness rather than light'. So he sent his Son to be the light of the world, the light that was to shine in that darkness and not be overwhelmed by it. 'The true light that gives light to every man was coming into the world.'

The ancient world knew all about darkness. When the sun set, darkness reigned, and in the absence of moonlight that darkness was total. To experience that nowadays means a journey somewhere very far from towns or roads or houses. Then we may sense something of the oppressive, almost frightening, power of darkness, as it seems to push in on you, squeeze you, bind up your eyes. To the ancient world, at least, darkness was an unconquered enemy.

But Jesus had come to conquer the darkness. He was not a reflector, but himself a source of light. And for lives that open themselves to him, he becomes 'the light of life'—life-giving light.

A reflection

All that light has to do to dispel the darkness is to shine. All the darkness has to do is to be open to the light.

A prayer

Lord Jesus, light of the world, shine into the dark corners of my life, showing me what is there and helping me to bring it to you for cleansing. Amen.

A way to pray

Self-examination: What are the dark areas of my life?

Thanksgiving: That God has sent Christ to be the light of my life.

Meditation: To reflect on the ways in which the light of Christ can reach every part of my life.

MONDAY
Lost

'The Son of Man came to seek and to save what was lost.'

Luke 19:10

For five years my work took me all over three of England's loveliest counties—Oxfordshire, Berkshire and Buckinghamshire. Often I found myself driving down unfamiliar country roads to tiny villages where I was going to speak to the Church Council or a group involved in some area of mission. In the winter it was dark. Clutching the directions I'd been given over the phone, I would turn off the main road and head into no man's land. 'You can't miss it,' the vicar had said cheerfully, 'It's right next to the church.' He was right, you couldn't miss it . . . in broad daylight. But when the whole village is totally dark, with no street lights and clouds obscuring the moon, the church, in common with everything else, is wrapped in inky darkness.

Consequently I got lost. Indeed, the last five years have been a continuous investigation of the nature and properties of lost-ness. Does one press on, hoping aganist hope that what is fairly obviously the wrong road will miraculously turn into the right one? It's astonishing how often I did that, optimism triumphing over experience. Or does one, more rationally, turn the car round and go back to the last familiar landmark, and start again?

Being lost is an odd condition. You don't stop being who you are, of course. Sat there in my car, miles from anywhere, I am still the husband of Christine and the father of Philip, Rebecca and Adrian. I am still the Bishop's 'officer for evangelism'. I am still the priest in charge of Ducklington. But at that moment I'm no use to any of them! A lost person or article is still 'what it is', still valuable in itself, but in the wrong place, disconnected from its purpose and unable to be or do whatever it is intended to be or do.

And that is what Jesus meant when he said that people were 'lost'. All of his illustrations of it bear that out. The lost sheep was valuable, but outside the fold. The lost coin was valuable, but no use to anyone while it was lost somewhere in the house. The lost son was loved by his father, but sitting among the swine in a 'far off country' the relationship could never be what it was intended to be. When the Bible describes people as 'lost' it isn't 'putting them down' but asserting their value. We don't talk about a 'lost' piece of rubbish or a 'lost' handful of grass. To deserve the description 'lost' something has to have value to start with.

So even when we are lost we are still valuable to God. Indeed, we are so valuable that he sent his Son on a 'search and rescue' operation for us. After all, that's almost exactly what the words of Jesus in today's reading say: 'The Son of Man came to seek and save what was lost.' The initiative is entirely his, but, unlike a lost coin or a lost document, we have to contribute something to that rescue operation. The lost son had to 'come to his senses' (Luke 15:17) and recognize his situation. Like me in my car, he had to stop hoping that he would somehow suddenly not be lost and retrace his steps to the point where he had taken a wrong turning.

But when he did the father ran to him. God is looking for his lost sheep. And in Jesus he has done all that is necessary to rescue them and bring them home.

A reflection

It is bad to be lost, but it is even worse to be lost and not to know you are.

TUESDAY

Poor

'He has anointed me to preach good news to the poor.'

Luke 4:18

'Poor' is a miserable kind of word in English. Just think of the way we use it. 'She got a poor examination result.' 'He's in a poor condition in hospital.' 'She's a poor little thing.' 'A poor attempt... a poor stroke... a poor excuse...' and so on. It speaks of failure, weakness, frailty, even fault ('How do you explain these poor results?').

But the word used in the New Testament does not carry the same degree of contempt. It simply means 'poor'—without money. And specifically it carries the idea of dependence, of needing to depend on someone else. The usual Greek word for 'poor' is connected with the word for 'beg'. And it was no disgrace to be poor, unless it had come about through laziness.

Indeed, it is a recurring theme of the Old Testament that the poor have a 'special place' in God's favour. He exercises (in the modern jargon) an 'option for the poor'. Almost every reference to the poor in the Psalms or in Proverbs, for instance, speaks of God's care for them and of their blessedness in being thus dependent on him. God 'rescues' the poor, God 'hears their call', God 'provides for the poor', he 'maintains the rights of the poor and oppressed'. Not only that, but it is the poor who 'seek God', who 'will see and be glad' (Psalm 69:32).

It's easy to hear the echoes of all this in the teaching of Jesus. 'Blessed are you who are poor, for yours is the kingdom of God'

27

(Luke 6:20). It is the poor who are invited to the banquet of that kingdom, the poor to whom good news will be preached.

There's no doubt that Jesus felt a special affinity for the poor people of his day—the literally poor, who lived in hovels, had little to eat and went around in rags. Many lived by begging. They knew what it was to be dependent on the generosity of others. That was what distinguished them from the self-sufficient, confident people around them, who made their plans, built their extra barns and felt no need of support from anyone.

The good news for the poor was not that Jesus was going to initiate a new economic system, or overthrow the unjust structures that created and perpetuated their poverty, but that their poverty helped them to understand something that the rich can never know, or only know with great difficulty (like the camel through the eye of a needle). What they knew was how to receive gifts. They were beggars, and knew it, while the rest of us think we are self-sufficient, but aren't.

Jesus was not saying that poverty was a good thing, or that we should not work to eradicate it, but that the hungry and penniless are loved by God and can depend on him in a way that those with riches cannot understand.

In the Beatitudes, in Matthew's Gospel, the saying about the blessedness of the poor is slightly expanded: 'Blessed are the poor in spirit, for theirs is the kingdom of heaven.' Here the spiritual message is clear. The 'poor' are models for the disciple not in their material poverty but in their sense of humble dependence. The 'poor in spirit' humbly trust God, even when to do so costs them much in worldly status, wealth or power. The kingdom of heaven belongs to those who depend on its king.

A reflection

To have any chance of getting through the eye of the needle (whatever the phrase means) the camel would have to be stripped of its load. Excess baggage is usually a problem!

A prayer

Heavenly Father, help me to learn to depend on you alone, and not on what I own, or what I can do, or who I am. Amen.

For discussion

The Bible tells us to care for the poor and weak, and also to learn from them. Does that create a contradiction for Christians as we address the problem of poverty in the modern world?

Fear

'But I will show you whom you should fear: Fear him who, after the killing of the body, has power to throw you into hell.'

Luke 12:5

'Fear' is a very special word in religious language. We are called to 'fear' God, and that idea worries many modern people. I remember getting a letter from a popular journalist and poet objecting to my use of the word in relation to God. 'How,' he asked, 'do you equate telling people God loves them and then that they ought to fear him? Doesn't perfect love cast out fear?'

And in one sense he was right. The Bible does say that perfect love drives out fear, and it says it specifically about our fear of God (see 1 John 4:18, also Luke 1:74). We are not meant to be anxious and afraid before God if we are living in his love.

But that does not remove the requirement to 'fear' him in a more fundamental sense—the sense expressed in the verse at the top of this chapter. God holds all the issues of life and death, of sin and judgment, of time and of eternity, in his own hands. To realize that is to regard him with awe and respect . . . yes, and 'fear', in the sense of a healthy recognition that he is the ultimate determining factor in the whole universe.

There is an unavoidable tension here, which has troubled Christians all down the years. God loves us, and gave his Son for us. Through him we can enter into a relationship which is close, confident, even intimate. We can 'know' him. We can call him *'Abba'*. We can be sure of his love for us. Through Jesus Christ, creatures can know and love and be accepted by their creator. And this means that there has always been a strand in Christian devotion that emphasizes our assurance, confidence and intimacy with God.

On the other hand, God is still God. He 'dwells in light unapproachable'. He is the wholly 'Other', the source of holiness itself: 'in him there is no darkness at all'. Our status before him is always that of creatures—and of creatures who have failed to live by his demanding standards. It is we who have polluted his universe, caused hurt and pain to others, lied and cheated and indulged ourselves. So that 'if we claim to be without sin, we deceive ourselves'. If God is perfect goodness, we are far removed from him, even in our best moments.

So there has also always been a strand in Christian devotion that emphasizes our creaturely dependence on his mercy and our need to approach him with reverence and awe. We 'fear' him in the sense that we recognize who he is.

The element that brings these two ideas together is the love of God. The One who made us—our ruler and judge—is also and at the same time the One who loves us so much that he gave the life of his Son for us. The One who has indeed power to destroy evil is also the One who went to such lengths to save us from the consequences of our own evil. 'God did not send his Son into the world to condemn the world, but to save the world through him.'

We are neither called to abject fear of God, nor to crass familiarity with him. To 'fear', in the biblical sense, is not incompatible with love. It is to see him for what he is.

▊ A reflection

God dwells in light, but he sent his Son to bring that light into our world.

Treasure

'For where your treasure is, there your heart will be also.'

Matthew 6:21

'Treasure' is a romantic word to most of us. We read *Treasure Island* when we were children, with its daring attempt to find buried riches on a remote island somewhere. There is something fascinating about the idea that somewhere, perhaps near us but out of sight, there is hidden wealth 'beyond the dreams of avarice' (as they say).

When Jesus spoke of 'treasure' he certainly included that idea—think of the parable of the man who found treasure in a field and went to enormous lengths to make sure that it became his. But he also spoke of treasure as the thing we value most. The word in Greek—*thesaurus*—means a casket, the thing in which we store what is valuable to us. So, in this saying of Jesus, he is speaking of that inner casket, that storehouse of the spirit, where we hide away from the sight of others those things which are most precious to us.

And what they are determines the whole direction of our lives. That is the point of the saying. Our 'heart' follows our 'treasure'.

Some people live their lives for money. If they do, it's usually quite obvious. Some have as their 'treasure' something less easily recognized: the garden, a collection of porcelain, their public reputation. We may successfully hide these from others, so that they seem like harmless hobbies or even praiseworthy ambitions. But the one who keeps the treasure knows! To eat and sleep and drink the garden, or to put all our energy and concern into our collectables, or to care more than anything else in the world that we should be respected and honoured: these are the symptoms of the treasure-keeper.

Jesus has an answer to these distracting obsessions. Get a new and good one! We all need to have goals and ambitions, or our lives lack direction and purpose. But trivial or unworthy goals lead to a trivial and unworthy life. So why not set yourself (he says) the highest of all goals? Go for the best 'treasure' of all. 'Store up for yourselves treasure in heaven, where moth and rust do not destroy, and where thieves do not break through and steal.' And the rationale for this is precisely the point that our goals determine our journey: 'For where your treasure is, there your heart will be also.'

There is nothing sadder than a life with no purpose, but close behind it is the life with an unworthy purpose. If we really live for sport, or a hobby, or the acquisition of wealth, then in the end we are doomed to disappointment, because these concerns are earth-bound . . . as mortal as we are. But to store up treasure in heaven—to 'seek first God's kingdom and his righteousness'—is a worthy goal, a treasure worth gathering and keeping.

▊ A reflection

'My Saviour has my treasure', says the hymn. So pleasing him will be my ambition.

▊ A prayer

Lord, help me to get my priorities right and to go for the best treasure of all. Amen.

▊ For discussion

What role can, and should, 'lesser' ambitions have in our lives? How can we stop our interests and hobbies becoming obsessions and priorities?

FRIDAY

See

'Come, and you will see.'

John 1:39

'Seeing is believing', we say. But it is only partly true. I can see the illusionist sawing a woman in half, but I don't believe it. Conversely, I can't see radio waves, but I am about as certain as I could be that they exist. Still, by and large it's true. The evidence of our own two eyes is very convincing. Don't just tell me, show me.

And that was the evidence Jesus offered to his first two prospective disciples. They had been followers of John the Baptist, but he had told them very clearly that Jesus was now the one they should follow. He was 'the Lamb of God, who takes away the sin of the world'. He was the one who would baptize, not with water, but with the Holy Spirit.

So they literally followed Jesus—when they saw him passing by, they fell in behind him. Jesus turned round to see them, and asked what they were looking for—a question we've already considered. They didn't answer that question, but put another one: 'Rabbi, where are you staying?' Perhaps they wanted to imply that their interest was not in a brief encounter, but a longer-term commitment; not a conversation by the roadside, but real discipleship.

Whatever they meant, the reply of Jesus was the words we are considering today: 'Come and see.' So he led them to where he was staying, but in fact he led them much further than that. He led them to abandon their trade and follow him. He led them to share in his work of preaching, teaching and healing. He led them to the shores of Galilee, the hot streets of Jerusalem, the entrance to Jericho, the dusty path to Caesarea Philippi. Following him would involve excitement, pain, despair, disappointment, triumph and joy. They may have thought they were going to look at his lodgings, but he was inviting them to share his life.

Jesus still says, 'Come and see.' That was his invitation to the apostle, Thomas, who wanted visual evidence to allay his doubts about the resurrection. But for those who cannot 'see' his hands and his side, there is still an invitation to 'see'. As Jesus pointed out to Nicodemus, you can't see the wind, but you can see its effects. We can't expect to see Jesus in his humanity and not many of us, one suspects, are going to see him in a vision, but we can 'see' his 'effects'. We can look at the evidence of the impact of Jesus in the lives of others—not only in the great saints of the faith, but in the lives of ordinary Christians, too. They are called 'witnesses', and witnesses speak only of what they have personally experienced. By looking at them we can see the impact of Jesus. Perhaps the Church should be more willing to say to seekers, 'Come . . . and see.'

A reflection

The invitation to seekers to 'come and see' will only have good results if, when they come, there is something worth seeing.

A prayer

Lord Jesus, help me to 'see' you in the lives of others and to recognize the marks of your presence. Amen.

For discussion

What opportunities can we make for people seeking Jesus to 'come and see'? And what pitfalls should we avoid in making that invitation?

SATURDAY

But

'Whoever believes in him should not perish but have eternal life ... God did not send his Son into the world to condemn the world, but to save the world through him.'

John 3:16–17

A word doesn't have to be long to be important. 'But' is a very short word, both in English and in Greek, yet it is crucially important in understanding the message of the New Testament. In fact, 'but' almost sums it up!

The picture of the world offered by the Bible is one of vivid contrast between the good earth that God created and the present disordered situation. God created the heavens and the earth, the sea and skies, the fish, birds, animals and, as the crown of it all, human beings. In the simple but profound words of Genesis, he looked at what he had made and 'Behold, it was very good.'

The second chapter of the Bible offers us a picture of that idyllic world, with the Man and the Woman set in a veritable garden of delight. The trees were not only fruitful but beautiful to look at. A river watered the garden—no need for back-breaking irrigation! Under the earth there was gold and onyx. As the writer might have added, 'What more could you ask?'

But ... but, as we know, they weren't satisfied. In this strange and haunting story of Eden, these beings made in God's image presumed to know better than he did. They wanted to be privy to his secrets, to experience both good and evil. In the language of the story, they 'ate the forbidden fruit'. We can let that stand for pride or presumption. They wanted to be 'like God'. They weren't content to be made in his image, stewards of his creation, lords of the good earth. They wanted equality with their creator. And in grasping at that, they lost everything. They destroyed the garden of delight for ever. Work, which formerly was satisfying and fulfilling, became a burden. Their relationship, previously one of mutual support and respect, became one of male dominance and female subservience. All the pressures and pains that we tend to think of as exclusively modern and contemporary are described in this ancient creation story in Genesis. The beautiful world made by God is no longer 'very good', but infected with evil.

All of that, of course, is only one side of the contrasting picture offered by the Bible. That is the dark side. *But*... but God did not cease to love his human creatures. They were still of infinite value, still made in his image, still objects of his love and concern.

So the 'other side' of the Bible's picture is the story of God's action within history to put right what had gone wrong, to restore what had been ruined and to find—as we have already thought—what had been lost. The human race may have wandered off into a far country, distant from Eden. But God has never forgotten us.

The motive for his concern comes out of the very heart of his nature. 'God is love', says St John—not just 'God loves' or 'God is lovely' but that he is love. What love is, God is. By our actions, in the words of St Paul, 'we were by nature objects of wrath'. Yet he goes on, 'But God, because of his great love for us, made us alive with Christ, even when we were dead in transgressions.' The argument may seem an odd one to modern ears, yet it can still speak powerfully to us. If we got our deserts, we would be the objects of God's anger. After all, it is we, not him, who have spoilt his beautiful creation with our wilfulness, pride and anger. *But*... but we are not objects of his wrath, but of his love. Today's verses, so familiar and perhaps therefore so easily taken for granted, put it with simple clarity: 'God so loved the world that he gave his one and only Son, that whoever believes in him shall not perish but have eternal life.'

You see, it all hinges on 'but'. The situation is dark and desperate, *but* God has not abandoned us. Evil and darkness often seem to hold sway in the world, *but* God has still got a purpose for his creation. Death shadows the whole of human life, *but* God has made us alive in Christ. 'But' represents the realism of the Gospel. It is not a message of empty hope, a kind of whistling in the dark. It faces the reality of the world as we know it, but recognizes that—in the end—'all will be well'.

A reflection

'But' is how we say that there's another way of looking at something.

A prayer

Lord, you have not made us for destruction, but for life. Help me not to be a slave to my failures, but to trust in your redemption. Amen.

For discussion

Take the story of the Garden of Eden and try to give it a contemporary setting. What is the 'forbidden fruit'? What are the consequences of rebellion? How do those 'curses' express themselves in modern-day life?

The way, the truth and the life

Jesus answered, 'I am the way and the truth and the life.'

John 14:6

This saying is often used to support a doctrinal assertion about Jesus Christ—that he is the unique revelation of God and the only way to him.

But in context, it was probably not intended principally to be a doctrinal assertion, but a reassurance to the disciples that in the doubt and confusion that inevitably lay ahead there was a clear divine purpose. They might feel that they did not know 'the way', or were struggling after 'the truth', or were anxious about what lay ahead on that journey to the 'Father's house'. Do not be anxious or upset, Jesus tells them. You may not know the answers, but you do know me. You believe in God. Well, put a similar kind of trust in me.

Jesus is the way to the Father. Following him brings the disciple eventually not to him, but to the Father. He doesn't just show us the way, like prophets and preachers. He is the way. In other words, he is not like a signpost ('This way to God'), but a pathway to the Father. Commit yourself to the pathway and you will get there.

Jesus is the truth about God. He explains this a few verses later: 'Anyone who has seen me has seen the Father.' If we want to know what God is like, what his standards are, what demands he makes of us, then look at Jesus. There can be no clearer picture of God: this man was transparent to his qualities—the life and character of God shone through him. That is the claim, and we must decide whether all that we know of Jesus supports it.

Jesus is the life of God. All through the Gospels we see Jesus giving people 'life'—enhancing lives, restoring lives, even raising people from death. The Holy Spirit is called the 'life-giver', but on earth Jesus also took on that function. As he moved through the crowds and touched the lives of people here and there, his touch was a touch that gave new life. In the Fourth Gospel the supreme illustration of that is the story of the raising of Lazarus—a kind of preparation for the story of the resurrection of Jesus himself. From the cruel darkness of death, out of the stench of the tomb, loosed from the grave-clothes that were the trappings of a corpse, Lazarus was called by Jesus into the light of day. The story speaks of many things, but above all it speaks of the miracle of life and the power of the life-giver.

A reflection

If Jesus is the way, the truth and the life—what else can I possibly need?

A prayer

Lord Jesus, help me to follow your path, believe your truth, and live your life. Amen.

A way to pray

Self-examination: *Have I sought other ways? Other truths? Another kind of life?*

For thanksgiving: *That God has given us in Jesus such a marvellous picture of himself.*

Meditation: *Picture Jesus as a pathway to the Father. What obstacles do I see on the path? What things about it may cause me to hold back? What is there at the end of the path that drives me onwards?*

Truth

The law was given through Moses; grace and truth came through Jesus Christ.

John 1:17

Jesus answered, 'I am ... the truth.'

John 14:6

You stand in the witness box, clutching a slightly grubby copy of the King James Bible (I sometimes wonder if the legal authorities are not sure if any other version really 'works'). You are told to read out the words on the card: 'The evidence I shall give is the truth, the whole truth and nothing but the truth.' Because it is required, you do it. But anyone who thinks about it for five minutes will come to the inevitable conclusion that what you have sworn simply can't be done—not by a human being, anyway. We can do our best to tell the truth. We can promise to tell the truth as accurately as we can remember it. We can even banish any thought from our minds of omitting anything or holding anything back.

But the truth, the whole truth and (especially) nothing but the truth? It is asking more than we can promise to deliver.

Most human beings recognize that the whole idea of 'truth' is a very slippery one. That very great BBC correspondent, Gerald Priestland, in his book *The Dilemmas of Journalism*, remarked that any journalist who promised you 'the truth' about something was inevitably lying. The 'truth' is slippery and elusive. Do we mean the 'facts'? Or the consequences of the 'facts'? Or deductions that some people have made from the 'facts'? A more cynical broadcaster at the BBC once remarked to me that whenever a politician says 'The fact of the matter is . . .' (and they say it very often), you should start counting the silver.

In ordinary, everyday experience, too, we are aware how often what seemed to be the 'truth' of the matter turned out, in the end, to be nothing of the kind. The fact that we believed it to be the truth at the time is irrelevant. We were not guilty of deception, but we were wrong.

I think it is because of all this that people sometimes fight shy in the spiritual realm of claims to a knowledge of absolute truth. Our experience of life tells us that 'truth' is most often a mixture of greys, not a matter of black and white. So when Christians claim that God has revealed the 'truth' in Jesus Christ, or that he is 'the truth', or that we can 'know the truth' (all ideas to be found in the Fourth Gospel), they tend to be very sceptical.

However, the most common word in the New Testament for 'truth' (*aletheia*) is not principally about perfect knowledge of the 'facts'. It is much more than that. It means the reality that lies at the core of appearances—the 'truth' in the sense of the essence or heart of the matter. Now while that is, in one sense, much more than knowing the 'facts', it actually makes a different kind of demand on our credulity. It asks us to believe that the source of this truth has a truer knowledge of things, or perhaps a better understanding of them, than is available elsewhere. It speaks of an integrity of understanding, seeing things whole.

The problem for humans about 'truth' is that each of us has a limited view of it. We are limited by time—we don't live very long. We are limited by space—we are greatly affected by what we call our 'environment'. We are limited by our capacity to understand—we may be brilliant experts in one sphere and totally ill-informed about another (think of the professor of science whose seven-year-old understands more about football!).

The only one we can conceive of who is not limited in these ways is the One who made us, the eternal, infinite God. The 'truth', in this sense of integrated understanding, grasping the reality that lies at the core of appearances, can only be known by God, in the end. And that means that we can only know it if he reveals it to us.

And that is the claim that is made by the Bible: not that we mortals can have a kind of hot-line to perfect knowledge, but that God has shown us in Jesus all we need to know, all the truth that our finite minds can comprehend. And that this 'truth' is the reality that lies behind the appearance of things, the essence of the matter. It is in that sense that Jesus, the Son of God, is the 'truth'—he puts us in touch with reality. It is this truth that opens our inner eyes, gives meaning and purpose to existence, and (in the words of Jesus) 'sets us free'.

A reflection

Knowing the truth is not the same as knowing the facts.

A prayer

God, you are the source of all truth. Help me to know all the truth that I need to know now, and give me the assurance that one day I shall know all the rest as well. Amen.

For discussion

People often ask whether Christianity is 'true'. What do you think they mean by this? And how would you try to answer the question?

Way

Jesus answered, 'I am the way ...'

John 14:6

In the modern world we are used to walkways, clearways and motorways and most of us still know what a pathway is. However one decorates the word—or the object—a 'way' is still the means of getting somewhere. You can put an escalator on it, or divide it into traffic lanes, or lay metallic tracks and call it a railway. Whatever you do, it is still the means of getting somewhere. From the dawn of history, and I'd guess from the very beginnings of language, 'ways' were important.

The countryside is still criss-crossed with 'ways'—footpaths, bridleways, sheep tracks. They climb up the sides of mountains and follow ancient rivers. They lead to fords, or markets, or towns. People once travelled them only on foot or horseback. We do it in the Cavalier or the Metro. But however you use it, a 'way' is how you get somewhere.

The saying of Jesus of which 'I am the way' is a part was in response to one of the commonest human questions: 'How do I get there?' Jesus had told his disciples that he was 'going to his Father's house' to prepare a place for them. He would return and take them to be with him there, so that they could be where he was. The prospect, I suppose, was slightly alarming, slightly reassuring. And then he added, 'You know the way to the place where I am going.'

They didn't, that was the trouble. I imagine the disciples looking at each other, waiting for someone to have the courage to ask the obvious question. As so often, it was Thomas who put the problem into very simple words.

'Lord, we don't know where you are going, so how can we know the way?' If we aren't clear about the destination, it is impossible to know the route to it. 'My Father's house' was a bit vague. Did he mean heaven? And if so, why didn't he say so? It was all very mystifying, they felt—and Thomas put their misgivings into a direct question.

To which, of course, he got a direct answer.

'I am the way...'

I don't imagine it was the kind of answer they expected. In its full form ('I am the way and the truth and the life. No-one comes to the Father except through me') it simply asks them to trust him. Instead of a complicated set of instructions—the spiritual equivalent of 'Go straight down the road, turn left at the post office and take the third turning on the right after the letter box'—he offered them a personal guide, himself. In the idiom of his day, 'I am the way' meant 'I'll take you there.' But, of course, you'll have to trust me. Like the guide who leads you through a wilderness or across a mountain, he had to be trusted implicitly. He can only be the 'way' to those who believe that he knows where he is going and how to get there.

'Way' is a lovely word in English, almost always full of positive feelings. 'We're on our way,' we say. 'Where there's a will, there's a way.' Equally in the Greek of the New Testament, '*hodos*', the way, is a very positive word. At its simplest, it just means 'path' or 'track', and as we have seen they were essential elements of life in a rural, and in places wild, land. The shepherd, in the great Psalm of David, guides his sheep along 'paths of righteousness'—more literally, the 'right paths'. God's law, in another Psalm, is the 'light for our path'. Everyone knew that it was essential to keep to the path and not to wander off into the dangerous areas of precipice or pit.

Not surprisingly, it also came to mean a course of action, a pathway in the sense of a route to a chosen destination. And then it acquired a more abstract meaning, as a way of thinking, a pathway in the sense of an approach to things or a way through them. At its most vivid, it was used in the early days of the Christian Church as a title for those who had chosen to follow Jesus. They were 'followers of the way' and Christianity was simply (with a capital 'W') 'the Way' (Acts 9:2; 19:9). What is so good about that title is its sense of movement. The Christian Church was on a journey—the same journey, really, as Jesus had told his disciples about. They were following him, or travelling in his company, on the journey to the Father. It was a dynamic movement that had a 'way' and a destination.

Perhaps we need to recapture some of that sense of commitment to a journey. Possibly modern Christianity has become too static, too much involved in maintenance, in building plant and putting down roots, to enjoy to the full the sense of a journey. Journeys are exciting and often rewarding, but they can also seem threatening and disturbing. It may be that this sense of discomfort holds us back from full commitment to the unpredictability and excitement of the 'way'?

If so, the answer for us is exactly the same as it was for Thomas and the disciples. 'I am the way.' We do not know—and cannot know—the details of the journey that lies ahead of us. But we can and do know who is leading the way, our companion and guide on the journey. Jesus said, 'I am the way . . .' 'And surely, I am with you always, to the very end of the age' (Matthew 28:20).

A reflection

To arrive without having travelled is to miss out on the full experience.

A prayer

Lord Jesus, you are the way. Keep me on the path. Illuminate it with your presence. And give me the strength to complete the journey. Amen.

WEDNESDAY
Life

Jesus answered, 'I am ... the life.'

John 14:6

What is 'life'? We speak of people being 'full of life'. We say, 'Where there's life there's hope.' And when things go a bit contrary we shrug our shoulders and mutter, 'That's life.'

As a matter of fact, those three ways of thinking of life are quite different. When we say 'Where there's life, there's hope', we mean that while a person is still alive, still breathing, there's hope that they will recover. Life, used in that way, means biological life, the common possession of animals and human beings.

When we say 'That's life' we mean 'That's the way things are'— life as a matter of human existence. The Greeks had a word for it, '*bios*'—the root of all those complicated words beginning 'bio—' You can find it used in that way in the First Letter to Timothy, where Paul speaks of living 'peaceful and quiet lives'.

When we say someone is 'full of life' we certainly mean more than that they're just alive! I suppose that somebody who is 'empty of life' would be dead, but many of us who are definitely alive wouldn't necessarily describe ourselves as 'full of life'. So the phrase recognizes that there are degrees of 'being alive' and a person full of life has, at that moment, a heightened awareness of what it means to be alive—they're enjoying the experience of life to the full. And that is the sort of life which Jesus offers to us.

The most usual word translated 'life' in the New Testament is '*zoe*'—again, recognizable as a prefix to many technical words in English, such as 'zoological'. As the biblical writers use it, it normally means more than simply 'being alive', in the animal sense. It refers to life as a principle, life in the absolute sense. At its highest, it is life in the way God is alive—what we think of as 'eternal' life.

It is this life—not just 'being alive'—that Jesus came to make possible for human beings. So he said to his Jewish critics, 'You diligently study the Scriptures because you think that by them you possess eternal life. These are the Scriptures that testify about me, yet you refuse to come to me to have life' (John 5:39–40). Religious people seek the secret of 'eternal life'—life beyond death, life with God for ever. It's not surprising that they should look into the sacred writings to see if it can be discovered there. Jesus, however, wanted to point not to a set of principles or a code of conduct, but to himself. 'As the Father has life in himself,' he had told these same critics earlier in the same dialogue, 'so he has granted the Son to have life in himself.' In other words, God has life in the absolute sense, and is able to grant this same quality of life to his Son. But, more than that, he has given to Jesus the power to grant it to others. As Jesus said, 'I have come that they [his 'flock'] might have life, and have it to the full.'

This is not quite as mysterious as it sounds! The life that God has is 'eternal', not just in the sense that it 'goes on for ever' but in the sense that the life of God is the source of all other life. Without him there would be no life at all. And it is 'eternal' because he is eternal, without beginning or ending, 'being' rather than 'becoming'. Natural life is, of course, the gift of God, but that life comes to an end through the due processes of time. Eternal life is also the gift of God, but it is much, much more than natural life. Eternal life is sharing in the life of God himself, being alive in the sense that he is alive, and eternal because it is rooted not in the natural, passing order of things but in God himself.

'This is eternal life,' said Jesus (again, in the Fourth Gospel), 'that they may know you, and Jesus Christ, whom you have sent.' And the significance of 'knowing Jesus Christ' is, as he has just said, that God has granted him authority over all people 'that he might give eternal life to all those you have given him'.

'Life', in this sense of the word, is therefore a gift, exactly as natural life is. We don't have to earn the right to be born. So far as we are concerned, it simply happens, and at the time we are unconscious of the event. Eternal life is also a gift, which this same Gospel has likened to being 'born again'. You can't earn a gift. We can't earn the right to eternal life. But God gives it to those who 'come to' his Son.

All through history people have sought the 'secret of life'—'Life, the Universe and Everything', as *The Hitch Hiker's Guide to the Galaxy* called it. The heart of the Christian good news is in the words of Jesus that we are looking at today: 'I am the life.' The 'secret' has been revealed. The 'mystery' has been made known. Life, in this absolute sense—the very life of God himself—is offered as a gift by God to those who turn to his Son.

A reflection

Eternal life is not so much about duration as quality.

A prayer

Grant me, Lord, that inner life which comes from your life, and mirrors your character. For Jesus Christ's sake, Amen.

For discussion

What is the purpose of life? Some would say it is simply to 'live it'. Others would say that it lies beyond this life. Must life have a purpose at all?

Forgiven

'Friend, your sins are forgiven.'

Luke 5:20

Forgiveness is one of the loveliest ideas, and being forgiven one of the loveliest experiences, connected with being human. Because we are human, we fail—we let people down, offend or hurt them, behave in ways that cause us shame. But to be forgiven means that that failure has been put away and we can go back to where we were before we failed.

In ordinary human experience, forgiveness is often extremely difficult. People say, 'I'll forgive him but I'll never forget what he did.' And that, of course, is not forgiveness at all. Or they feel that the offence is so great that it is beyond forgiveness: 'that was unforgiveable behaviour', we say... and sometimes, sadly, we mean it.

In any case, forgiveness without repentance is incomplete. Nothing is really achieved if we simply say the words to an offender, 'I forgive you.' For forgiveness to be real it requires two actions—repentance on the part of the offender, forgiveness on the part of the 'victim'. Unconditional forgiveness might give the impression of condoning the offence.

So forgiveness can't be given lightly, or it means nothing. True forgiveness is a wiping out of the past. What is truly forgiven can never be brought back. In the language of the Bible it is placed 'as far as the east is from the west' (Psalm 103:12).

The Greek word normally used for 'forgiveness' in the New Testament conveys this sense of 'distance' very well. It literally means 'to send away'. The sin that is forgiven is 'sent away', dismissed, completely removed from the scene. As spoken by Jesus it is a word of forensic significance. What is forgiven is taken away and the person who has been forgiven is set completely free. Today's words of Scripture are from the story in the Gospels of the paralysed man who was let down through the roof of a house where Jesus was staying. His friends, despairing of getting through the crowds, climbed on the roof and lowered him down in front of Jesus. As the spectators awaited a miraculous healing, Jesus said to the paralysed man, 'Friend, your sins are forgiven.' The bystanders were shocked (only God could forgive sins—so who was this upstart?). The friends were probably very surprised. They'd had no idea that the paralysed man needed forgiveness before he needed healing.

In fact, the forgiveness seems to have been the clue to the healing, because very soon he was on his feet, picking up his stretcher and walking off, liberated both inwardly and outwardly. That's the effect real forgiveness has on us. It sets us free from the chains of the consequences of our own behaviour.

In the ministry of Jesus he 'sent away' all kinds of sins—those of the woman taken in adultery, those of the paralysed man, those of the woman 'who was a sinner', even the thief crucified beside him on the cross and the soldiers who carried out that unjust deed. He 'sent away' what we should call 'trespasses'—breaches of God's holy law. They could now be forgiven. He 'sent away' what the New Testament calls 'sins'—failures to live up to God's moral standards. He 'sent away' or cancelled 'debts', while requiring his people also to cancel the debts owed to them. Forgiveness, in this sense, is like a great flood of cleansing, making right what had been wrong and putting what is evil far away from its victims.

But there is another word for 'forgiveness' in the New Testament. It's frequently used by St Paul. Based on the word for gift (*charis*), it speaks of the act of forgiveness, that generosity, whether human or divine, that makes it possible for offenders to be forgiven. Perhaps the most beautiful expression of it is in the

Letter to the Ephesians (4:32): 'Be kind to one another, tender-hearted, forgiving one another, as God in Christ has forgiven you.'

This word for forgiveness emphasizes forgiveness as 'gift'. You can't demand to be forgiven. Someone who has the right to do it has to decide to exercise it on your behalf. It is, in other words, an action of grace.

But it also speaks of the generosity of God in his great act of forgiveness in Jesus. In ordinary, day-to-day Greek the word means to bestow a favour without any strings attached. That is a glorious picture of the way God forgives us. While we were still sinners, says St Paul, Christ died for us. God wasn't waiting for a response before he acted. In a marvellous, cosmic gesture of love he sent his Son to die for the forgiveness of sins.

It is true that we must repent to receive that forgiveness, but no other condition is set—no matter the size of the sin or the consequences of what we have done. Forgiveness is an act of grace, a favour without strings: in the simplest language of all, a gift.

And as we are forgiven, so we forgive.

A reflection

To err is human, to forgive divine.

A prayer

Lord, help me today to be aware of how wonderful your act of grace is in forgiving me, and grant me a deep sense of gratitude for it. Amen.

For discussion

People are often asked whether they are prepared to 'forgive' someone who has done them a terrible wrong—perhaps even murdered their child. How would you answer that question if you were in that situation?

FRIDAY
Freedom

'He has sent me to proclaim freedom for the prisoners.'

Luke 4:18

'Freedom' is one of the great words of this century. Virtually all the former colonies of the Western powers have received their freedom. Those who were once slaves have received not only legal freedom, but increasingly freedom from those unwritten restrictions which human beings use to create underclasses. Women have begun to experience freedom to work and study and fulfil themselves in ways that few were able to do in the past. Everyone's in favour of freedom, it seems.

Yet few people, in my experience, feel free. In our daily lives, in our relationships with one another, in our work and even in our leisure pursuits, we still feel ourselves in a kind of bondage. Things are expected of us. Demands are made. We feel trapped by circumstances. In law we are probably the most 'free' people who have ever lived. In practice, far too often we still feel like slaves.

So when Jesus says that he has come to proclaim 'freedom for the prisoners', or promises that 'if the Son of Man sets you free you will be free indeed', we hear him speaking our language, too. Unlike many founders of great religions, he didn't come to heap a new set of requirements on us—more rules to keep, more rituals to observe—but to set us free. If that is really what he has promised, and if he can really fulfil it, then his message is truly 'good news' of a quite unique kind.

In the Greek world in which the Gospel was first preached slavery was, of course, the norm. It was argued (as it was in nineteenth-century England) that the economy could not prosper without vast numbers of slaves to provide economical labour. But sometimes a slave would have his or her slavery put aside. They would be given their 'freedom'—often as a mark of gratitude by their owner. Because the slave could not pay for his own freedom, this was effected by a legal fiction. The law required either that he pay for his freedom, or be sold to another owner. So he was sold to another owner—one of the gods. The money was paid into the temple treasury by his previous owner in the presence of the slave, and then a document of sale was drawn up containing the words 'for freedom'. He could never be enslaved again, because he was now the property of the god. He had been bought, but only in order to be set free.

That is the picture St Paul uses to illustrate the freedom which Christ 'buys' for his people—you can find it in Galatians 5:13, for instance. And once he sets us free, we cannot be enslaved again. We 'belong' to him, we are his willing 'slaves'—a word the early Christians loved to use to describe themselves. So it is true: 'if the Son sets you free, you will be free indeed'.

But that freedom is bought at a price. It always is, whether it is the blood of 'freedom fighters' or of great pioneers of human freedom like Gandhi and Martin Luther King. The freedom of God's people—the 'glorious liberty of the children of God', as Paul puts it—is also bought at the price of blood. 'It was not with perishable things such as silver and gold that you were redeemed [that is, set free] ...' writes St Peter, 'but with the precious blood of Christ, a lamb without blemish or defect' (1 Peter 1:18–19). He was thinking of the sacrificial lamb offered for sins in the Law of Moses, where 'without shedding of blood there is no remission of sin'. There is no need to think in crude terms of Jesus bearing the wrath of God. More simply, God in his love for us sent his Son to be the means of redemption—the key to real freedom—for all those who put their trust in him.

This inner freedom is a great, transforming force for good. It sets us free from the shackles of the past and liberates us to be the people God intends us to be. As Charles Wesley put it in his famous hymn, 'My chains fell off, my heart was free; I rose, went forth, and followed thee.'

A reflection

To serve someone we love, and who loves us, is not slavery.

A prayer

Lord, set me free from the inner shackles of sin and the outer shackles of taboos and regulations, and release me to serve you in perfect freedom. Amen.

For discussion

It took the Christian Church over 1,900 years to agree that slavery was immoral. Are there areas where God's creatures are still in other kinds of slavery, from which they need to be released?

Peace

'Peace I leave with you; my peace I give you.'

John 14:27

In the Communion service in our church, as in most nowadays, we mark the 'Peace'—a moment when the congregation greet each other and say, 'The peace of the Lord be with you.' Of course, some use words of their own—I've heard, 'Hello, fancy seeing you here!' and even, 'Hope you've got over the tummy bug.' Despite this, it's supposed to be an oasis of shared peace right at the heart of the liturgy.

But in our case, during the 'Peace' the children come back in, jumping and running and pushing to get to their parents, waving the bits of drawings or models they've made in their own groups. In some ways, it's the most chaotic part of the service, and yet I think we all recognize that this, too, can be a sharing in the 'Peace', because those children represent our shared life, something that binds us together and makes us one. And that is the heart of the biblical meaning of the word 'peace'.

In Hebrew it's '*shalom*'—still the normal greeting among Jews in Israel, of course. '*Shalom*' means peace, but it also means wholeness, salvation, being truly one with yourself, with your neighbour and with God. And for the Christian, real peace is nothing less than that.

Jesus left 'his peace' with the disciples. The promise is there, in today's verse of Scripture. But the next words in the Gospel qualify it: 'I do not give to you as the world gives.'

For the world, 'peace' is the absence of war. Frequently, the world's peace is the result of conquest—the *pax Romana* was the peace imposed on the countries the Romans had conquered. It was peace, of a kind—'Peace', as T.S. Eliot put it in *Murder in the Cathedral,* 'but not the kiss of peace.' Peace, in ordinary experience, is the absence of noise, strife, conflict. In other words, it has a kind of negative quality. You define it by what it isn't.

The peace of Christ is the exact opposite. It isn't determined by the 'absence' of anything. As Jesus told these same disciples, 'In the world you will have trouble'—but they would still have his peace. They could retain his peace in the midst of turmoil, persecution, raving crowds, menacing monarchs and all the rest. Because the peace he gave was not to do with circumstances, but with inner tranquillity. It is not about the sort of place the world is around me, but the sort of person I am in that sort of world.

His actual phrase for it is disarmingly simple: 'In me you will have peace.' In me. It's as simple in Greek as it is in English. Yet it is very profound. What does it mean to be 'in' him?

Jesus saw those whom the Father had given him—his 'little flock'—as being united to him as he was to the Father. They were and are one with him, one 'in' him. So as part of him they can begin to share the qualities that he has, including this sense of peace. It is, we notice, 'his' peace which he gives to them, rather than simply 'peace' in the general sense. It is peace as he understands it—not the peace of conquest, or the peace of absence of noise or conflict, but the 'peace that passes all understanding', the peace that comes from knowing that in the end all will be well, because in the end the purpose of God will be fulfilled, and that is perfectly good.

And yet Christ's peace is, in one sense, the peace of conquest. For part of his promise to the disciples has all the confidence of the conquering king. 'In this world you will have trouble'—there is no escape from the way the world is, in terms of the here and now. 'But' (that marvellous word again!)—'take heart! I have overcome the world' (John 16:33). In Christ—and only in Christ—we can share in the peace that follows victory. The battlefield may still be smoking, there may be undetected mines around us, stray units of the enemy may be hiding out somewhere: but peace can rule in the hearts of his company, because they know that the conflict has been decided and light has conquered darkness. 'Lift up your hearts!'

A reflection

Peace is not decided by external circumstances, but by inward tranquillity.

A prayer

Lord grant me your peace—the peace that comes from knowing that you have overcome the world. Amen.

For discussion

Peace is more than the absence of war—but can it ever be less than that? And if it includes an absence of war, should all Christians be pacifists?

THE THIRD SUNDAY IN LENT
The gate

Jesus said . . . 'I am the gate for the sheep.'

John 10:7

A gate has many functions other than its obvious one of being a way into a field. It can be closed, and keep the animals in—and predators out. It can be opened, and let the animals out—as Jesus said, to 'come in and go out and find pasture'. Without a gate, a field is a prison.

Speaking to a largely, if not entirely, rural audience, Jesus could expect to be immediately understood. If he was the 'gate of the sheep' (that is, of the sheepfold), then he had these two functions. He would protect his flock, by keeping from them the 'predators' that would destroy them. And he would lead them out into places of pasture and cool water.

Israel had a tradition of thinking of the king as a 'shepherd' of his people. Again, this was a dual image. The king protected the nation—God's people. He shut the gate to enemies and invaders. But he also provided for them: it was his responsibility to see that people had food and work. In the days of the good kings, the people were safe and prosperous. In the days of the bad kings, enemy followed enemy in over-running the land, and there was often famine as well.

Jesus was the Shepherd King of Israel. And not just of Israel, because 'I have other sheep that are not of this sheep pen.' He is the protector of his people, not so much in the ordinary ups and downs of life—no one is immune to accident or illness, for instance—but in the ultimate sense of the battle between good

61

and evil. No one can pluck his sheep from his hand. They are his, and he takes responsibility for them.

And he feeds his sheep. He leads them out into broad pastures where they can find good food. He nourishes us with himself, the living bread. He is the water of life—the life-giving water—for our spirits. The 'gate' of Christ safely keeps us in and leads us out into abundance.

A reflection

I may not like to think of myself as enclosed in a sheepfold, but it is very reassuring to know that Jesus is its gate, keeping out what is harmful and giving me freedom to go beyond its confines with confidence.

A prayer

Lord, when I feel anxious or threatened, show me again the gate of the sheepfold, barring evil from harming me. When I am spiritually dry or hungry, show me the open gate leading to pastures and springs of water.

A way to pray

Self-examination: *Jesus said, 'Take no anxious thought for tomorrow.' So why do I endlessly worry about things that haven't happened yet, and probably never will?*

Thanksgiving: *For the gate of the sheepfold, protector and provider for his people.*

Meditation: *Reflect on the role of the gate of the fold as it is seen by the sheep. What is most reassuring about it?*

MONDAY

Repent

'Repent and believe the good news!'

Mark 1:14

One of the best-known caricatures of Christian witness is the man in the shabby raincoat holding a banner that reads, 'Repent, the end of the world is nigh.' In fact, so well known is the picture that I assume millions of people think those words are actually in the Bible. Of course they aren't. They emerge from some collective memory of cartoonists.

But 'repent' is in the Bible, I'm afraid. I suppose most of us wish that it wasn't. We associate it with feelings of guilt, with impending punishment and a requirement to grovel. And modern people, even more than their ancestors, don't believe in guilt, are a bit ambivalent about punishment, and positively hate the idea of grovelling.

In fact, the biblical word is much more positive than all that. To repent is to 'change your mind': not alter your opinion or adjust your stance, but in a root-and-branch way undergo a real, deep and lasting change of mind. It reflects a total reversal of attitude, a complete transformation of our view of something.

To repent, in the Christian meaning of the word, is to accept that our view of a matter is wrong, and God's view is right. In other words, it's a frank admission that God was right all along. It may be connected with feelings of guilt (or it may not). It may involve our being punished (or it may not). It certainly involves humility, but not grovelling. Because to repent is to do something that only beings made in the image of God can do. And repentance releases us from a moral cul-de-sac into the life God intends for us.

The moral cul-de-sac is the road of self-justification. It's the way most of us respond to the probings of conscience. I have (let's say) been unfair to a junior colleague at work. At times this has troubled my conscience. 'What you did,' it says, 'was unkind, unjust, hurtful... in short, wrong. So come along, admit it.' My response is to engage my conscience in a kind of dialogue. 'I admit it wasn't like me to react like that,' I concede. 'Nonsense,' says conscience, 'it was exactly like you when you're under pressure. You always did take it out on those weaker than yourself. Remember your little sister?' 'But that's simply not true,' I counter. 'My typist needed to be taught a lesson... for her own good. Perhaps I went a bit too far, but it was understandable.' But conscience doesn't back down (note: she never does!). What was done was wrong. God says so, and you know it. And I do, deep down, but I won't admit it. My action was out of character, ill-judged perhaps, even a mistake. But definitely not a sin.

Repentance breaks this pointless dialogue and gets me out of the cul-de-sac, because, when I repent, what I am doing is agreeing with God. Instead of trying to justify myself, I accept his verdict. What I did was wrong. He is right. And I am truly sorry.

To repent is to turn the key to blessing. All through the New Testament, it is those who repent who are forgiven, accepted, made God's people and inheritors of his kingdom. The reason is simple. We are created to do the will of God and we shall never become whole and happy people apart from it. So while I am resisting his will I am holding back his blessing.

Repenting and believing are two sides of the same action. To repent is to turn from what is wrong. To believe is to turn to what is right and put your trust in it. So the baptismal promise is to 'renounce evil' and 'turn to Christ'.

No one can repent for us. Organizations and institutions can't 'repent'—only the people who belong to them. *People* repent, or refuse to repent. Conscience can push, the Holy Spirit can convict of sin, but only the human will can respond by repenting. But when we do repent, then we are free to believe the 'good news'. In fact, it is double good news: that sin—admitted, repented—can be forgiven and that we can be free from its clutches. As the old hymn says, 'Be of sin the double cure: cleanse me from its guilt and power.'

A reflection

God wants us to repent so that we can be whole and happy people—not to make us grovel.

A prayer

Lord, show me if I need to repent of anything—and help me not to argue!

For discussion

Do you find it difficult to admit it when you have done something wrong? If so, why? Have you ever repented after a real struggle? If so, what did it feel like?

Believe

Jesus answered, 'The work of God is this: to believe in the one he has sent.'

John 6:29

'Believe' is a strange word, used in English in many different ways. To the question, 'Is James in the garden?' it would be possible to answer 'I believe so'—and mean by that that there was some doubt about it. At the other extreme, one can imagine a loyal mother in a juvenile court assuring the magistrates, in the teeth of all the evidence to the contrary, that she still 'believed' that her son was a good boy at heart. We 'believe' that the moon is round, that Tokyo is the capital of Japan and that Julius Caesar once landed in Britain, but many of us have no personal proof of any of those statements.

So when the Christian faith asks us to stake everything on an issue of belief we may understandably be confused. What does it mean to 'believe in God', or to 'believe in Jesus Christ'? Is it just a balance of probabilities (like James in the garden)? Or a pronouncement of blind hope (like the mother in court)? Or a repetition of what we have been told is a scientific or historical fact (like the roundness of the moon, the location of Tokyo and the exploits of Julius Caesar)?

In fact, when Jesus used the word 'belief', or invited people to 'believe' in him, or in the gospel, he wasn't speaking in any of those categories. The word the New Testament uses for 'belief' could more helpfully be translated as 'trust' or (as the New English Bible consistently renders it) 'have faith in'. To believe (in this sense) means to place our confidence in or rely upon someone or something. It has very little to do with mere credence—believing that something is so.

John's Gospel uses the verb 'to believe' no less than ninety-nine times, often on the lips of Jesus himself. He calls people to 'believe' in him—in other words, to put their confidence in him, to rely upon him, to trust him. The issue is not so much what do they believe *about* him, but whether they are prepared to commit themselves *to* him.

So it is absolutely right that in the baptism service of the Church of England (and many other churches) the candidate is asked, 'Do you believe and trust in him?' To believe God exists is a valuable and necessary first step—and one which, according to the apostle James, even the demons have taken! But the great turning point is when we are willing to put our trust in him.

It's an old story, but like all old stories it makes a very telling point. The famous trapeze artist of a previous era, Blondin, was about to push a wheelbarrow on a tightrope across the Niagara Falls. He asked the journalists standing by if they believed he could do it. With one voice, they all assured him that they believed he could. But when he invited one of them to climb into the wheelbarrow to provide a passenger for this strange exploit, they all declined. They believed, but they didn't have enough confidence in him to put their lives (literally) on the line.

Human nature finds it hard to trust another—a scepticism born of hard experience, I fear. We all know what it is like to be let down by someone we trusted. On the whole, we would rather be told how to earn something, how to pay the going price, than be asked to trust somebody's promise. So, in the incident from which today's words of Scripture are taken, the question put to Jesus was, 'What must we do to do the works God requires?' Just tell us what is necessary, and we'll do our best to pay the price and earn his approval. The answer they received probably both surprised and disappointed them. There was no price to pay and no way of earning his approval . . . except to 'believe in the one he has sent'— Jesus himself. They had to trust that God's Son could give them living bread from heaven (v. 35) and that he alone could 'raise them up at the last day' (v. 54). These blessings simply cannot be earned. They can only be received on the basis of trust. That is the simple key to understanding what it means to believe.

▌ A reflection

To believe something is a decision of the intellect. To believe in someone is a decision of the heart.

▌ A prayer

Lord, I believe. Help me where faith falls short.

▌ For discussion

Christian 'faith' involves accepting certain things as 'true' (for example, the life, death and resurrection of Jesus, and that he is the Son of God). But it also involves putting our trust in him—having confidence that he will keep his promises, for instance. How do these two aspects of faith hold together for you? And in which area are you more inclined to have doubts?

WEDNESDAY

Receive

To all who received him . . . he gave the right to become children of God.

John 1:12

There is one absolutely authentic saying of Jesus which is not in the Gospels: 'It is more blessed to give than to receive.' St Paul reminded the Ephesian elders of it ('remembering the words the Lord Jesus himself said'), so it was obviously well known in the early Church but failed to find a place in the Gospel narratives. At first glance it states the obvious—clearly it is more commendable, more deserving of honour, to be a 'giver' than a 'receiver'. But Jesus said more than that. He actually said it was more 'blessed'—literally, a happier thing. Giving makes us happy—happier than simply being recipients of other people's generosity. That's an interesting thought and not at all obvious!

Yet Jesus tells us to receive—indeed, that only those who 'receive' him will have the right to become 'children of God'. It may be more 'blessed' to give than to receive, but obviously it is also essential sometimes to be prepared to receive rather than to give.

The word the Gospels use for 'receive' can mean either simply to 'take' or in a more formal sense to 'receive' . . . not only things, but people, the Word of God, mercy, even eternal life. It suggests an openness to them—the kind of openness that enables us to receive a guest into our home, for instance. The opposite of 'take' may be 'give', but the opposite of 'receive' (in this sense) is probably 'reject'.

And that is the context of the saying of Jesus in today's verse of Scripture. The people of his day, 'his' people, did not receive him. In fact, they rejected him. The popular acclaim which welcomed the healer from Nazareth turned to scorn and then rejection when they discovered the true nature of the claims he was making. 'He came to that which was his own' (his own race, his own land, his own culture, his own religion), but his own did not receive him'. It was that rejection which is the setting of the promise that follows. For, in contrast, 'all who did receive him', 'those who believed in his name', were given the right to 'become children of God'.

Another word for this kind of receiving is 'accepting'—welcoming without reservation. Jesus offers himself to people, and people can and do reject or accept him. The very action of offering himself creates the need for a response, because we have to decide what we are going to do with this offer: accept it, or reject it. God's great gift of his Son is unconditional, in the sense that it is an offer to all. But it is not unconditional on the human side, because we have the fearful and God-given privilege of choice, and we can reject the offer. The tragedy of the Gospels is the rejection of the Messiah by most of his own people, but that tragedy is repeated every time a human being, faced with the offer of God's love in his Son, rejects it.

Sunday by Sunday Christians approach the Lord's table and hold out their hands to receive bread and wine, the sacramental signs of Christ's offering of himself. Very simply, we take and eat, we receive the cup and drink. Nothing could more vividly portray the sheer simplicity of receiving. A child could understand it. God offers us his love, forgiveness and acceptance in his beloved Son. And he offers it as a gift. We reach out and welcome it, accept it, receive it . . . and with that love, we receive the right to become his children.

▌ A reflection

It is more blessed to give than to receive; but sometimes it is much harder to receive than it is to give.

A prayer

Lord, I am not worthy to receive you, but only say the word, and I shall be healed.

For discussion

What are the obstacles to accepting Jesus Christ? Is it fear of the consequences? Doubts about the nature of the offer? Pride, because we want to 'earn' whatever we get? Or just that it seems too good to be true?

Follow

'Follow me, and I will make you fishers of men.'

Mark 1:17

For Simon and Andrew, partners in a small fishing business, it seemed like any other day. Except on the Sabbath, the routine was always the same—out during the night fishing, then ashore in the morning to unload the catch and try to sell it. When that was done, there was maintenance to do—usually on the nets, sometimes on the boat. Only then could they think of a few hours rest and sleep before the whole business started over again. Fishing may seem a restful and restorative hobby, but as a job it is unremitting, risky and very hard work. Galilee did not lightly surrender its riches.

But this was not 'any other day'. This was to be the day that would change their lives totally. Because as they were casting their net—presumably in an effort to increase the day's catch—Jesus came near. They knew him already—that much is clear from John's account of these early days of Christ's ministry. They were probably very impressed. They had been disciples of John the Baptist, and he had told them that Jesus was the one who would 'baptise with the Holy Spirit', the 'lamb of God who would take away the sin of the world'. So they were more than just interested in this new and impressive prophet from the nearby village of Nazareth.

Still, it must have come as something of a shock when he said to them, 'Come, follow me, and I will make you fishers of men.'

The first part of the invitation is clear enough: 'Follow me'— become my followers, as once you 'followed' John the Baptist. The imperative 'Come' adds a note of urgency—they were to do it now. But a strange promise was added, and it's interesting to speculate what they thought it meant. If they accepted this invitation to follow Jesus, he would make them 'fishers of men' . . . literally, of 'people' (*anthropon* in Greek—human beings).

At the moment they were fishers of fish, if you see what I mean. Now their horizons were to be expanded. Instead of affecting the temporary destiny of fish, they would be involved in the eternal destiny of human beings. They were to be moved from the tiny, limited, repetitive stage of the shores and waters of Galilee to the vast arena of human destiny. In other words, life would never be the same again.

And, of course, it wasn't. They couldn't possibly have imagined what lay ahead: wonders and marvels beyond the wildest dreams of these devout men. They would glimpse heaven on the Mount of Transfiguration. They would experience bitter sorrow, disappointment and failure. They would share the agony of Gethsemane, the horror of Golgotha, the exquisite joy of Easter day. They would travel far beyond their native land with the message of salvation, and become, in the end, martyrs for the cause. As Peter himself wrote many decades later, they would have to suffer many kinds of trials but would also be filled with an 'inexpressible and glorious joy'.

'Follow me', said Jesus, 'and I will utterly transform your life.' It is an invitation and a promise that he still makes. The conditions are the same, the urgency is the same, the promise is the same. To 'follow' is to go the same way as the leader, and that way leads via the cross and resurrection to the Father.

A reflection

To follow someone you need to keep them in view, go at their pace, and walk in their steps. Above all, you have to believe that they know where they are going.

FRIDAY
Obey

'... teaching them to obey everything I have commanded you.'

Matthew 28:20

In my childhood, obedience was a great virtue. 'Disobedience may seem fun,' my mother used to say, 'but it is a risk to run.' Children were certainly taught to obey, rather than question, what adults told them. And then, during my National Service in the Royal Air Force, I learnt an even sterner lesson in obedience. Orders were to be obeyed without question and in all circumstances—however unreasonable they might seem. Thus former generations were schooled in the habit of obedience to authority: parental, educational, institutional and ecclesiastical. I don't recollect, as a child, ever discussing the Christian faith. We were taught it, and our duty was to obey what we were taught.

To modern readers that must all sound medieval. Children learn by discovery. People must be given reasons for their choices. Authority is to be distrusted: by its very nature it tends to corrupt. Apart from obeying road signs and traffic signals, the very concept of unquestioning obedience is foreign to most people's experience.

So it must seem strange to find that the last command of Jesus to his disciples was to tell people to 'obey everything I have commanded you'. His gospel is not an invitation to a debate but a call to surrender arms.

The basis of this command comes earlier in this speech (which is known as his 'Great Commission'). 'All authority in heaven and on earth has been given to me,' said Jesus. 'Therefore go and make disciples of all nations.' God has given authority to Jesus, and Jesus was giving authority to the apostles—authority to teach and to call people to obey God.

They were to 'make disciples'. A 'disciple' is, literally, a 'learner'. As Jesus had gathered his disciples, who sat at his feet and drank in his words, so the disciples, having learnt, were to become teachers and themselves gather disciples. But they were still to be disciples of Jesus, not of his followers. The call is for us, too, to gather at his feet and learn from him, to drink in his words and model ourselves on his life.

That is a vital part of the obedience of a disciple. The word in Greek means not just to learn from someone but to become their adherent—imitators of the teacher. So it is not only the words of Jesus that shape his disciples, but all that he is, and was on earth: his strength, his concern for others, his openness and honesty, his courage and gentleness. When we set out to 'obey' Jesus we are asking to be shaped by him in our thinking and our actions.

This is a long way from the call to blind obedience that marked the pupil and the soldier of former times. With our eyes wide open we respond to the call to follow Jesus, and then he invites us to be his disciples: to enjoy the privilege of receiving his wisdom, insight and love and of being 'conformed to his image', as St Paul put it. This is willing obedience, freely entered into, which sets us free to be fully and completely human. To decide to obey him is to liberate myself from the chains of self-will and discover the freedom of God's children.

A reflection

Christ's service is perfect freedom.

A prayer

Heavenly Father, help me to lay down the arms of my rebellion and for love of my Saviour to obey his just and gentle rule. For his name's sake, Amen.

For discussion

Compare obedience to a tyrant with obedience to a loving parent. What difference does it make to the way we exercise obedience? In daily life, what does it mean to set out to obey 'all that Jesus commanded'?

Live

> **'Man does not live on bread alone, but on every
> word that comes from the mouth of God.'**
>
> **Matthew 4:4**

Of course, we do live on 'bread', on food. A foster-mother in our village received a child of eighteen months who weighed less than twenty pounds, because he simply would not eat. The doctors and health visitors were baffled, but they knew that if he could not be persuaded to start eating he would inevitably die. Prayer and loving care did persuade him to start eating, and I can recall the exciting moment when his foster-mother announced that he had put on eighteen ounces in a week. Food nourishes life, and without it we can't survive.

But the point of this biblical saying—which Jesus quoted from Deuteronomy, in the Old Testament—is that it is not all that 'man' needs. People need bread, but they need more than bread. Life is more than mere existence, even comfortable existence, and here Jesus is concerned with that extra element that turns survival into real life.

'Man'—and once again the Greek word is *anthropos*, 'person', 'human being'—also lives by the word of God. That's a strange and profound saying, and it deserves a closer examination.

'Every word that comes from the mouth of God' sounds very explicit, and I believe it is. In its Old Testament context, it clearly refers to the 'commands of the Lord', many of which the wandering Israelites had conspicuously broken. But these commands, Moses explained to them, were for their good. They were the discipline of a loving and caring parent, whose ultimate purpose was to bring them into a good land, with 'streams and pools of water, with springs flowing in the valleys and hills; a land with wheat and barley, vines and fig-trees, pomegranates, olive oil and honey; a land where bread will not be scarce and you will lack nothing' (Deuteronomy 8:7–9). The commands were 'words from the mouth of God', but so were the promises.

Moses was anxious that the Israelites should not become proud in their new-found wealth and prosperity and forget the Lord. When they had more than enough 'bread' to live by, he wanted them to know that true life involved more than that. It involved recognizing the source of their satisfaction. It meant praise and thanksgiving for the generosity of the heavenly Father. When they had that balance right—when they 'ate their bread with glad and sincere hearts' (like the early Christians in Acts 2:46)—then they would truly 'live'.

It is a balance we need to achieve in the modern world, too. For 'bread' read food, by all means, but also read all the other things by which we try to live—success, sex, money, power, achievement. We, too, cannot live by these alone. On their own, they are an inadequate menu for people made in the image of God. They need the deep nutritional supplement of 'every word that comes from the mouth of God'—God's truth, in other words, however and wherever it is revealed to us.

A reflection

You have been born again, not of perishable seed, but of imperishable, through the living and enduring word of God.

A prayer

Lord, speak—and make me listen. Amen.

For discussion

In what ways does God's truth come to us now? How can we recognize it as 'the word of the Lord'? And what are the ways in which we can set ourselves to 'live by it'?

The vine

'I am the vine.'

John 15:5

Again we have a metaphor from rural life—and the rural life of the Mediterranean area at that. So perhaps we may not feel able to relate to it very easily. However, we can understand that the grapes depend on the life of the branches, and the branches depend on the life of the whole vine—root and trunk, as we might say. Jesus says, 'I am the vine.'

In other words, if the object of the exercise is to produce fruit, the success of the exercise depends on the life of the whole vine and the extent to which the branches of the vine can draw on that life. It can be put even more simply: the life of the Christian depends on the life of Christ. 'Without me, you can do nothing.'

Vines draw their sustenance from the soil. Jesus draws his life from the very life of God. The life that flows through him and into the Church and the individual believer is also the life of God himself. To receive it, we have to 'remain' in him—'abide in him' is the old translation. We have to make our dwelling with him, root ourselves in him. The quality of our lives as Christians is not determined by what we can do, but by the extent to which we are drawing on the life of Christ.

At one level that sounds obvious. Yet it is an elusive lesson for many of us. It is so easy to detach ourselves from him, from his will and purpose, and to become independent, self-motivating religious activists rather than dependent disciples. The moment we begin to think we can do it . . . we can't.

The vine which is Christ is healthy and able to sustain the life of all its branches. It is also well able to produce 'fruit'—the fruit of the Spirit, the fruit of changed lives.

A reflection

Don't be fooled. 'Without me you can do nothing.'

A prayer

Lord, when I am tempted to go off on my own, show me what it means to remain 'in Christ'. Amen.

A way to pray

Self-examination: *What are the ways in which I set out to strengthen my connection to the vine? And are there ways in which that 'connection' has become looser than it should be?*

Thanksgiving: *For the rich, abundant, satisfying richness of the life of the vine.*

Meditation: *Visualize a vine—soil, roots, trunk, branches, fruit. Imagine the sap flowing through its veins. Then think of yourself as a branch in that vine. Experience the flow of the sap. Allow it to reach every part of your being. And think of the fruit that is to come.*

Abide

'Abide in me as I abide in you.'

John 15:4 (NRSV)

'Abide' is not a word that trips easily off modern tongues, which may be why most recent Bible translations are at great pains to avoid it. 'Stay', 'remain' or 'dwell' are words that they prefer. But for me, at least, they don't have the force of 'abide'—and, what is much more important, don't convey the full strength of the word which the New Testament uses. One only has to consider the other words that have been used to translate it to see how elusive the idea is: continue, endure, stand, tarry. To 'abide' in a place is, of course, to stay there—to make it, even if only temporarily, your 'abode'. The New Testament uses it in that simple, literal sense—the two disciples on the road to Emmaus invited Jesus to 'abide' with them, because night was falling. And from that simple invitation came one of our best-loved hymns, 'Abide with me, fast falls the eventide'. But it also, and more often, uses it metaphorically, both of some quality dwelling in us (like faith, hope and love, in 1 Corinthians 13) or of the Word of God, the Holy Spirit or Christ himself making their 'home' in us.

The context of today's words of Scripture is, of course, the famous discourse by Jesus about the vine. He is the true vine, and his Father is the gardener. The Father's one intent is to produce fruit from the vine and in order to do that he prunes the branches to ensure that the energy of the vine is not wasted.

'I am the vine,' says Jesus, 'you are the branches.' If a branch is to bear fruit, all it has to do is 'remain in'—'abide in'—the vine. If it abides in the vine, then the life of the vine will abide in it. But apart from the vine, the branch is useless, dead and unproductive.

But this 'abiding' is not a totally passive occupation. If it were, then there would be no point in Jesus telling his followers to 'abide' in him. To 'abide' in him is to ensure that we remain connected to him in a dynamic way, so that his life—the 'sap' of the vine—can flow into us and produce fruit. For the branch of a tree that simply means hanging there, I suppose. But for the Christian it involves much more.

To 'abide' in Christ is to live 'in' him, to dwell in him, to make our 'abode' in him. He calls us to make our home with him. This speaks of a quite extraordinary degree of intimacy. He has opened himself to us in such a way that we can actually live in him, experiencing his presence all the while—not just when we are engaged in religious activities. It's exactly like living with someone: they become a constant factor (for good or ill!) in your life. As Jesus had already promised his disciples, if they loved him and obeyed his teaching he and the Father 'will come to him and make our home with him'. That is the true meaning of 'as I abide in you'.

This was the discovery made by Brother Lawrence back in the seventeenth century. He worked as a lay brother in the busy kitchen of a monastery in France. In the noise, heat and activity of the kitchen, he discovered the presence of God, just as real—indeed more real, for him—as in the silence of the chapel. He had discovered the secret of living 'with Christ', in a continuous experience of his presence. Like a branch, but more actively, he dwelt in the vine that is Jesus, and from that vine he drew the strength that he needed. His book of meditations and letters is called *The Practice of the Presence of God*, and that is exactly what he did—'practised', developed, actively sought to strengthen the reality of the interdependence of the vine and its branches.

The word 'abide' includes the notion of 'continuing'—you can't 'abide' for five minutes! To 'abide' carries the notion of a long-term residence, not a weekend stay. Certainly Jesus was asking his followers to become 'resident' in his love, to make their home in it. But he was equally promising to be a long-term 'resident' in their lives. Only by a continuous process can the strength of the vine be transferred to the branches, and then through the branches into the fruit.

In our own lives as Christians it's worth asking how much attention we pay to this idea of 'abiding' in Christ—'practising his presence', if you like. It requires time, commitment, faith and determination for the life of Christ the vine to be reproduced in us. Fruit doesn't grow overnight!

A reflection

The best fruit requires time, care and patience to produce.

A prayer

Lord Jesus, so that I may produce fruit to your glory, help me to accept the work of the divine gardener, even when it is painful or upsetting. Amen.

For discussion

In our own circumstances—at home, school or work, for instance—how could we begin to 'practise the presence of Christ'?

TUESDAY
Bread

'Give us today our daily bread.'

Matthew 6:11

In English, bread is sometimes called 'the staff of life', or at any rate it used to be, before it began to be rivalled by pasta, pizza, rice and other exotic foreign foods as the basic element of our diet. 'The staff of life' more or less sums up what the Bible usually means by the single word 'bread'—it's the thing that's necessary to support life, just as a walking stick or staff is to people who have a handicap or are tired on a journey. Bread sustains life—and if other cultures wish to substitute rice or pasta for bread, the principle remains the same: these are not luxuries, but necessities, the basis of the whole diet, and absolutely essential to the sustenance of life.

And God is the giver of bread. That is the first thing we need to know about bread, so far as the Scriptures are concerned. We are to be thankful for our daily bread and to see it as gift. And, in the teaching of Jesus in the Lord's Prayer, we are to ask God daily to give us bread—in other words, to recognize that the sustaining of our daily life is his concern. And notice that it is 'daily': that's to say, a regular provision, not abundance one day and scarcity the next. Each day God gives us the 'bread' for that day, the strength to live it. As I heard a one-hundred-year-old quote on the radio yesterday, 'As thy days, so shall thy strength be.' God's promised provision is as the need comes. He provides our daily bread. I remember a woman who lived in a town in Uganda during the terrible civil war there saying that every morning the family prayed, 'Give us this day our daily bread', and, as if by a miracle, every day they had just enough

85

to eat. 'I'd never realized before,' she said, 'how much that simple request could mean.'

But in the Bible bread stands for more, much more, than simply the provision of a daily calorie count. Bread sustains physical life, true. We life 'by bread'. But as God constantly reminded the Israelites, and as Jesus reminded his disciples, 'Man does not live by bread alone.' There is a 'bread' which sustains spiritual life, which does for our spirit what wheaten bread does for our body. And God is also the giver of this bread.

Jesus described himself as the 'bread of life'—'living bread', 'bread that gives life'. Just as ordinary bread is the 'staff of life', supporting us in our weakness, so he is the staff of spiritual life, giving us the strength to live and grow in the presence of God. Bread makes life possible; Christ makes spiritual life possible—he 'came down from heaven to give life to the world'.

So perhaps it's not surprising that at the end of his earthly life, in giving his followers a ritual action in which they could remember him and be strengthened, he chose bread as a vital element. 'After supper he took the bread.' On that occasion, of course, it was the unleavened bread of Passover, commemorating that great day when God brought Israel out of slavery in Egypt. But when he took it into his hands, it was simply bread, that very ordinary and common thing with which they were so familiar—the 'staff of life', the basic necessity.

And then he broke it. To 'break bread', in the culture of the ancient world, was to invite people to enter into a new relationship with you, as fellow guests at your table—indeed, as members of your extended family. If you had 'broken bread' with someone, they could never again be thought of as a stranger. In that single action, he united his disciples to himself in a new way—and he still does, every time we 'break bread' at his table.

Then he gave it to them to eat. It is such a simple gesture and yet so full of meaning. Being now members of his family, they were to share the family meal which he, as head of the family, had provided. His Father gave them 'daily bread'; their Saviour gives them 'bread from heaven'. From the one God they were to receive all they would need in terms of bodily and spiritual sustenance. As St Paul said, 'My God will supply all your needs.'

A reflection

It is the crushing of the corn that makes the loaf. It is the breaking of the body that makes the heavenly bread.

A prayer

Give us this day our daily bread, and give us too the bread from heaven. Amen.

For discussion

'Man shall not live by bread alone'—but he or she can't live without it. Can we offer people the bread of heaven if they do not yet have even the bread of earth?

Water

'Whoever drinks the water I give him will never thirst.'

John 4:14

A diet of bread and water is traditionally a punishment. It represents the minimum to sustain life—something simple and basic to eat, and water to drink. And, of course, the water is even more essential than the food, because without water a human being can't survive very long, especially in a hot climate.

Jesus said that he was 'the bread of life' but where water is concerned the wording is slightly—but significantly—different. He is the giver of water, its source, like a spring bursting out of the dry and parched ground. This is the imagery of the Gospels: Jesus likens himself to a source of water, cool and refreshing and inexhaustible. Nothing could have presented a more pleasing idea to his hearers.

It may be difficult for those of us who live in countries with an abundance of water (indeed, sometimes far too much of it!) to imagine the vital importance of water in the greater part of the world. Even a holiday in Umbria, in Italy, taught me the lesson, as the water supply failed, or was impure, and we tried to meet the needs of a modern lifestyle from plastic containers of water. In much of the world the 'rains' are simply the most important event of the year. Their arrival, with copious downpours, represents prosperity. Their failure means famine.

That was the situation in ancient Israel. Towns were built up around a well or a spring. Water was the determining factor in almost everything. Given water, life could survive and even flourish. Without it, even survival was impossible. So water became a synonym for what is essential to survival, that without which life is simply impossible. So the Jewish religion, like others in that culture, had festivals dedicated to celebrating water as a gift of God, and praying for a continued supply of it. It was at one such festival that Jesus raised his voice above the noise to proclaim, 'Whoever believes in me, as the Scripture has said, streams of living water will flow from within him' (John 7:38).

'Living water' is the opposite of stagnant or standing water, and therefore much the best and purest kind. Not only that, but living water from a spring was continuous and inexhaustible. If water is the very fountain of life, as human experience down the ages has seen it to be, then the claim of Jesus is that he provides a similar source for that inner life that is the life of God in us. The life he gives is continuous ('eternal', as the Bible calls it) and inexhaustible—it will not dry up or fail us at a moment of need.

Today's words of Scripture are taken from the dialogue between Jesus and the Samaritan woman at the well. He began their encounter by asking her to give him a drink from Jacob's well, but when she questioned the propriety of this he made this amazing claim to be able to give her—or 'anyone'—water which would satisfy human thirst for ever. Indeed, he offered more than that. The water he gave would itself become a spring within the recipient, giving them their own source of spiritual refreshment for ever—'welling up into eternal life'.

Water speaks to human beings of more than survival. Water cleanses, refreshes, renews. It enables crops to grow. It swells the grapes on the vine. It cools us when we are hot and relieves us when we are parched and dry. When Jesus says that he gives us the water of life, he is saying that the life of the spirit also needs cleansing, refreshing and renewing; that the fruit of the spiritual life needs this water in order to grow; that in the heat of daily life, when we are spiritually parched and dry, this is the water that we need. As the woman asked, 'Sir, give me this water.'

A reflection

The difference between a desert and a fertile valley is simply the presence of water.

A prayer

Lord, when I am dry, give me the water of life. When I am flagging, renew me with that water. And when I need cleansing, may that water wash me and make me clean. Amen.

For discussion

What can block the flow of spiritual 'water' into our lives?

THURSDAY
Spirit

'The Spirit will take from what is mine and make it known to you.'

John 16:15

'Spirit' is a strange word in English, but not so strange in the biblical languages of Hebrew and Greek, where in both it is the word for breath or wind. Sometimes, in fact, it is hard to tell whether it refers to 'Spirit' (with a capital S) or 'spirit' in the sense of character, or even breath or wind.

The well-known dialogue between Jesus and the Jewish leader Nicodemus is a case in point. Nicodemus came to Jesus at night, presumably to enquire about his teaching. What he learnt may not have been to his liking—that 'no-one can enter the kingdom of God unless he is born of water and the Spirit'. 'Water' presumably refers to baptism and 'Spirit' to the life of God.

But as the conversation goes on, the same word in Greek (*pneuma*) is applied to the wind, but as an illustration of the way that the Spirit of God works. 'The wind blows wherever it pleases. You hear its sound, but you cannot tell where it comes from or where it is going. So it is with everyone born of the Spirit.' The Spirit of God, in other words, is like the wind: you can't see the wind, which is literally invisible, but you can see its effects.

In Hebrew the word—both for Spirit and wind—is *ruach*, the hot, rushing desert wind which scattered the sand and made the tall grasses bow in its path. It pictures the power of the Spirit, not the 'gentle voice we hear, soft as the breath of even' (as the hymn puts it), but the surging impact of the gale.

And yet *pneuma* also means 'breath', and so we can equally properly think of the Spirit of God, as that hymn does, in terms of a gentle inner voice—like conscience—whispering the truth of God to us.

So there is no simple or single biblical picture of the Holy Spirit. He is like the wind, unseen but effective. He is like the desert gale, sweeping all before his path as he executes God's will in the world. He is the quiet breath of a whisper, speaking truth 'in the inmost being'. All are operations of the one Spirit, working to fulfil the purposes of God in the world and in people in many different ways.

And this is the Spirit Jesus promised to give to those who believe in him. It is this Spirit whom Jesus calls the paraclete, an almost untranslatable word which various versions render as 'comforter', 'counsellor' or 'advocate'. It literally means someone who 'stands alongside' us, like a counsel or advocate in court—someone who is 'on our side', representing our cause. So in one sense the old word 'comforter' can be quite helpful, so long as we don't think of it as a pat on the back! This 'comforter' encourages and strengthens us, rather than reassures us that everything is all right. He is an uncomfortable comforter, so to speak.

He also reveals the truth. This seems to be a primary task of the Spirit of God. In fact, Jesus calls him 'the Spirit of truth'—the Spirit who both is the truth and makes the truth known. As we say of him in the Creed, he 'spoke by the prophets'. Equally, he is the inspirer of the Scriptures, because it is his work to inspire the writers and also be the inspired interpreter of their words for the reader. 'All Scripture is God-breathed', says the Second Letter to Timothy—*theopneustos* in Greek, literally 'breathed out by God'. And there is that root idea again of the 'breath' of God at work in the Spirit.

It is also the work of the Spirit to represent Jesus in the Church and in the life of the Christian. The Spirit 'takes what is mine'—an odd phrase—and 'makes it known to you'. He will take what Jesus 'gives' him and reveal it to his disciples. Again, this is the Spirit as the interpreter of truth, the one who takes what may seem difficult, obscure or hidden and makes it known to us.

That is why the Christian needs the Holy Spirit—to explain the ways of God and make them clear. God does not want us to live in ignorance and he has given the Spirit to 'lead us into all the truth'. Every time we hear or read what we call the 'word of God' the divine interpreter is at work, opening minds and wills to the truth he wants us to know.

A reflection

We cannot contain or limit the power of the wind, but we can use it.

A prayer

Divine instructor, by your hidden life in me help me to know the will of God and the truth of God. Amen.

For discussion

Why is the Holy Spirit often spoken of as 'the forgotten member of the Holy Trinity'?

Share

'Come and share your master's happiness.'

Matthew 25:21

The word 'share' is not often on the lips of Jesus, but the idea of sharing is one that runs through his teaching and the life of the Church he founded. He invites us to share his life and his happiness. We are called also to share his sufferings and trials, his love for others, his rejection of evil. His cup is to be shared—'All of you, drink of this'—and the bread which he broke was for sharing, too. So although he didn't use the word a great deal, the principle is central to the Gospel, and we can see how true that is in the rest of the New Testament, where all the various words associated with sharing are applied over and over again.

The Christian life is, in essence, a 'partnership'—*koinonia*, in Greek. First of all it is a partnership with Jesus, a sharing (as we have seen) in the life of the vine, from which we draw our strength. Then it is a partnership with our brothers and sisters who believe. Faith and baptism take us into a new family, and that family is a working partnership. On the day of Pentecost three thousand people were baptized. The Book of Acts says of them that they 'continued in the apostles' teaching and fellowship'. They shared the common life. And they didn't think of that simply in terms of a 'feel-good' factor (as in 'there's a wonderful feeling of fellowship at our church'). It was a working partnership which had practical results. For instance, in those early days of the Church we read that the believers had 'everything in common'—they shared their money and possessions, so that no one was in need.

St Paul speaks of a 'partnership' or 'sharing' in the gospel, by which he means a partnership in the work of making that gospel known. He names many people who were his partners in this task. They shared together in the mission that Christ had given to his people. This is much more than a 'feeling', but I'm sure that from it came, as an inevitable side-effect, a wonderful sense of a shared calling, a shared task and a shared destiny.

The New Testament speaks of Christians sharing in Christ's death—St Paul says that he was 'crucified with Christ'. That's to say, we identify with his sacrifice and make it ours. But we are also given the privilege of sharing in his resurrection. That's to say, the life which the risen Jesus lived is also going to be ours. The secret is our identification with him.

Two of the disciples, James and John, once asked Jesus for a special favour—to sit on his right and left hand in the kingdom of heaven. Jesus told them that that wouldn't be possible, but if they were willing they could have the privilege of sharing in 'the cup' that he would have to drink and the 'baptism' he would have to undergo—presumably, his suffering and death on the cross. The message seems to be straightforward, if disturbing: to share in the triumph you have to share in the battle. There are no short cuts to eternal life. It is always reached by the same route, and that route goes right through Calvary.

A reflection

To share is to surrender something (my unique possession) in order to gain something (a shared experience).

A prayer

Lord, lead me away from a selfish clinging to things to a willingness to share: my joys, my hopes, my faith. Amen.

SATURDAY

Word

'Sanctify them by the truth; your word is truth.'

John 17:17

When the little green creatures from Mars—or somewhere a bit more distant than that—finally get here, how will we know whether to regard them as people or not? I suspect that one test would be: Do they talk? The ability to communicate in words is so distinctively personal that we would inevitably think of any speaking creature as a person. That is how important words are to us.

People are great verbalizers! Any teacher who has tried to stop a group of children talking knows that. To be forbidden to speak, or to lose the power of speech, or to become stone-deaf and unable to hear the words people utter, are fates we all dread. We love communicating and we love to receive communication. Perhaps that's why a baby's first words are so important.

So it isn't surprising that God, in whose image we are made, is the supreme communicator, nor that his first recorded activity was to speak: 'Let there be light!' And it was by a word that the whole universe came into being.

And it isn't surprising, either, that when God sent his Son into the world to represent him perfectly and carry out his purpose, he was given the title of the 'Word'—*logos*, in Greek. This expression has a particular meaning which goes beyond the idea of a noun, verb or adjective. '*Logos*' is the expression of a thought or concept, a saying, statement or speech. It is the whole idea, as it were—a complete expression, whether in one literal word or several.

Almost everyone knows the opening sentence of St John's Gospel: 'In the beginning was the Word, and the Word was with God, and the Word was God.' That is a very good, straightforward translation of an extremely profound statement. When J.B. Phillips, many years ago, wrote his paraphrase of the Gospels, this was how he rendered it: 'At the beginning God expressed himself. That personal expression, that word, was with God and was God.' Phillips is struggling to convey what the deceptively simple words of the Greek actually mean. The 'word' is the self-expression of God—the revelation of God. Through Jesus God communicated with the human race perfectly. That is what all words are meant to do, but so often we find our words are clumsily chosen or are misinterpreted, and so their true meaning is lost. God chose his word carefully, if I may put it like that. Jesus was—in the words of Hebrews 1:3—'the exact representation of his being'. He became on earth God's perfect 'icon', showing us the will and purpose of his Father.

So the 'Word of God', in its purest form, is Jesus. God spoke through the prophets, it is true, and through the moral Law, so that the Scriptures can properly be called 'the word of the Lord'. But that revelation is imperfect, in the sense that it is mediated to us through fallible human beings. The revelation through Jesus has no such fallibility. It is truly perfect. He is the 'Word of God' in a way no one and nothing else can ever be. As the Fourth Gospel puts it, 'No one has ever seen God. It is God the only Son, who is close to the Father's heart, who has made him known' (John 1:18, NRSV).

There is another word for 'word' in the New Testament, *rhema*. In the singular it means, literally, a word. In the plural it means speech. Its distinction from *logos* is that it denotes what is spoken rather than its meaning.

In his letter to Ephesus St Paul tells the Christians to take 'the sword of the Spirit, which is the word of God'. This is often taken by speakers to refer to the Bible, and I've even seen pictorial representations of the Bible as a sword (unlikely as that might appear). But in fact the word here is *rhema*, which can't possibly refer to the Bible as a whole but to a particular 'word' or utterance, presumably that part of God's revelation which the Spirit has provided us with in a specific situation in order to counter evil.

These may seem to be rather pedantic distinctions. God is a God who speaks, and what he speaks is his Word, whether it comes to us as conscience, as creation or as law. But he speaks his meaning, *logos*, most clearly in the person of his Son. God wants us to know and has gone to great lengths to let us in on the secret.

A reflection

Words can wound, and words can heal. So God's word sometimes causes us pain, but its purpose is always for our good.

A prayer

Lord, may I love, respect and receive your word, however and whenever it comes to me. Amen.

For discussion

If Jesus is God's 'Word', how can we know what that 'Word' says except through the record of it in the Gospels?

The good shepherd

'I am the good shepherd.'

John 10:11

Most people in the Western world have never met a shepherd. For that matter, neither have most sheep, at least in the sense of the shepherd in biblical times. So it's not surprising that most modern Bible readers, while very familiar with the word, find it hard to enter fully into the significance of the role of a shepherd in the ancient world.

That's a pity, because it is one of the most common metaphors in the Bible for a particular attribute of God—his tender and loving care for his people. Shepherds weren't (in Jesus' words) 'hirelings'—someone paid to do a job, and doing it reluctantly and without commitment. Shepherds cared for the sheep. Indeed, they virtually lived with them, which meant that shepherds were unable to join fully in the normal social and religious life of the community. They were a kind of race apart, living an almost hermit-like existence out on the hills, committed to the care, protection and well-being of their sheep.

That element of tenderness is particularly important. From the early days of Israel's understanding of God they had come to see him as holy, just, awesome, the great judge and ruler of all. But that great prophet of hope, rather awkwardly dubbed 'second Isaiah', introduces a quite new picture of God. Notice the vivid contrast between the 'Sovereign Lord . . . of power' and the gentle shepherd: 'See, the Sovereign Lord comes with power, and his arm rules for him. See, his reward is with him, and his recompense accompanies him. He tends his flock like a shepherd: he gathers the lambs under his arms and carries them close to his heart; he gently leads those that have young' (Isaiah 40:10–11).

This is a wonderful picture of God, and I'm sure Jesus had it in mind when he said of himself that he was the 'good shepherd'. He gives us the marks of that calling. He 'knows his sheep—and they know him'. They 'listen to his voice'. He is prepared to 'lay down his life for the sheep'. This is no superficial, sentimental kind of affection for the flock, but a total commitment to their well-being. It is wonderfully reassuring to know that that is how the Son of God regards the members of his 'flock'—the sheep who trust him and listen to his voice.

A reflection

We may not see ourselves as sheep, but it is still good to know that we have a shepherd.

A prayer

Lord, when I feel vulnerable, lonely and hurt, give me a sight of the good shepherd gently and tenderly caring for each member of his flock. Amen.

A way to pray

Self-examination: *Sheep can be stupid and wilful! In my own life, in what specific ways have I 'wandered away like a lost sheep'? What dangers have I drifted into through wilfully refusing to follow the shepherd's path?*

Thanksgiving: *For the daily care and attention of the 'great Shepherd of the sheep'.*

Meditation: *You are on a hot, barren hillside, tired, hungry and thirsty. The shepherd signals a move—you hear his voice. What may lie ahead? Dangers? Exhaustion? More heat? But you follow, because experience tells you that he knows what he's doing, and his only concern is your welfare.*

MONDAY

Kingdom

'The time has come,' he said. 'The kingdom of God is near. Repent and believe the good news!'

Mark 1:15

Most of us have a word we use very often. 'Basically' is one I hear a lot, especially from people being interviewed on the radio. Long ago, when I was a teacher, I remember one of my classes getting very giggly about something a boy was doing at the back of the classroom. On investigation I discovered he was keeping a record of every time I said 'significant', which was apparently my favourite word at the time. He'd clocked up seven instances already—and I hadn't been aware I'd said it once!

If Jesus had a favourite 'word' it may well have been 'kingdom'. At any rate, it could be said to sum up his message. Indeed, the 'kingdom' of God, or of heaven, was his message, the great truth he had come to reveal. He didn't just talk about the 'kingdom', he demonstrated it and—in a very important sense—he was it. 'If I by the finger of God cast out demons, then surely the kingdom of God is here,' he claimed.

So it's a pity that this word which Jesus used and valued so much seems so obscure to many readers of the Bible. In fact, enormous theological tomes have been written trying to explain its full significance! As most of us will never read them, there might be a danger that we shall fail to appreciate the very heart of the message of Jesus. We have made an essentially simple (but profound) concept into a theological 'problem'.

In the ancient world they were familiar with 'kingdoms' and 'kings'. The kingdom was where the king held sway: it was as straightforward as that. But the problem for us is to grasp what 'holding sway' really meant. The monarch had absolute power. His word was law. His decision was life or death. Judgments were settled before his throne. All authority resided in the king and that authority was total.

So when Jesus spoke of the 'kingdom of God' he meant, essentially, where God holds sway, where his rule is absolute. In one sense, of course, God is king of the whole universe, as its creator. But by his own decision he has given human beings the freedom to 'opt out' of his rule—we are not like the angels, programmed to do his will, but are free moral agents. He wants us to choose to obey him, to choose to love him. It's a vital part of being human.

So the kingdom of God in the teaching of Jesus exists wherever God's will is done—wherever people submit to his just and generous rule. And the reason Jesus 'is' the kingdom is that he came into the world for precisely the purpose of doing God's will. He said so, over and over again. 'I have not come to do my own will, but the will of him who sent me.' So Jesus proclaims the kingdom and shows us what it is like: it is life lived as Jesus lived it, in perfect harmony with the will of his heavenly Father.

The kingdom of God is good news. Being subject to the rule of tyrants like Herod or power-crazed emperors like Nero was obviously bad news. But to live our lives voluntarily under the rule of a king who loves us and whose only concern is for our ultimate good—that really is good news. And a community that lives like that is the kingdom of God.

The message of the kingdom tells us that it is possible to live in a new kind of society, by a new set of standards, under the freely accepted rule of a loving and wise God. Jesus calls us to enter into that society by repentance and faith, to wear its 'badge'—baptism—and to serve its purposes. It is the highest calling and the greatest privilege to be a citizen of the kingdom of God.

A reflection

'His service is perfect freedom.'

A prayer

Lord, help me today to be a loyal citizen of your kingdom, eager to do your will and fulfil your purpose. Amen.

For discussion

The standards of the kingdom of God are often in conflict with the standards of the 'kingdoms' of this world. Can you identify some of these points of conflict? How do we, and how does our church, stand in relation to them?

Happy

'Happy the pure in heart: they shall see God.'

Matthew 5:8 (JB)

We took our church's 'Tiny Tots' group to a mass picnic in the grounds of Broughton Castle, near Banbury. The event was very well organized by the Mothers' Union and included a short service at which the first song was that well-known ditty 'If you're happy and you know it clap your hands'. Later verses involved shaking bodies, jumping up and down and sundry other exhausting activities designed to leave the children in a state of quiet anticipation for the talk that followed. As the song ended, one mum remarked, 'Nothing very Christian about that!'

Now it's true that unbelievers—atheists, even—could sing a song celebrating 'happiness'. But for Christians it should have a particular and special meaning, because Jesus said that 'happiness', being truly 'happy', was a mark of God's kingdom.

The complication is that short word 'truly'. And the Beatitudes—those memorable sayings of Jesus which open the Sermon on the Mount—show how sharp the contrast is between the common perception of what it means to be 'happy' and what 'true happiness' is. Jesus said that the poor in spirit, those who mourn, the meek, the merciful, the pure in heart, the peacemakers and the persecuted are those who are truly 'happy'. That's certainly not how the world judges 'happiness'! A 'happy' man, in ordinary usage, is laughing, without a care, possibly even under the influence of drink.

I suspect it's that problem over the understanding of happiness that led most of the translators to prefer the more 'religious' word 'blessed' in this passage, but the fact remains that the Greek word *makarios* does simply mean 'happy'.

Jesus often said provocative, challenging things—things that make us re-examine our whole outlook on life. I believe this is an example of that dynamic use of language. 'You may think rich people are happy', says Jesus. 'Actually, those who know they are poor are the really happy ones.' 'You may think that people who are powerful and influential are happy. In fact, it is those who are meek who have the secret of true happiness.' 'You might think that people whose lives have been untouched by sorrow and bereavement are the happy ones. No such thing! The really happy are those who have been through the experience of loss and known the comfort and strength of God in it.' Jesus was carefully and deliberately turning upside-down the world's way of looking at happiness and offering another, better version—one that could survive disappointment, suffering, persecution and so on. And that, for Jesus, was the only 'happiness' worth having.

For the under-fives at our picnic, happiness was the open air, the sunshine, the sheer joy of jumping and shouting and laughing. There's no harm in that, and I have no doubt God smiles at it, too. It's good that they should know that God wants them to be happy. But as they get older they will come to know, God willing, that although life can't be one long laugh, it can have this inner happiness—'serenity' might be another word for it—that comes from joyful acceptance and humble gratitude. I think that is what Jesus means by being 'pure in heart'... and his promise is that those whose hearts are pure will 'see God'.

A reflection

Happiness based on my circumstances is by its nature temporary. Happiness based on my inner character cannot by its nature be taken away.

▌A prayer

Teach me day by day the secret of happiness—of joyful acceptance and humble gratitude. Amen.

▌For discussion

Think of examples of people whom you can regard as truly 'happy'. Are there common features in their approach to life?

WEDNESDAY

Father

'*Abba*, Father, everything is possible for you. Take this cup from me. Yet not what I will, but what you will.'

Mark 14:36

The New Testament is written in Greek, but the language of Jesus and his first disciples was Aramaic, a form of Hebrew. Just occasionally the Gospel writers retain a word or two of the Aramaic that Jesus spoke, perhaps when they feel that they can't adequately translate it. This saying, from the lips of Jesus during what is known as his 'agony' in the Garden of Gethsemane, is an example of that. '*Abba*' is the Aramaic word for 'father'.

Jesus called God 'Father'. Most Christians know that. He always spoke personally—'*my* Father'—as though to stress the particular relationship which he had with the first Person of the Trinity and to distinguish it from the relationship others can have through faith in him. Jesus was God's Son. By faith and grace we, too, can become 'sons of God'—but never in the sense in which Jesus was. Clearly his relationship with the Father was unique.

But while we can never become 'only begotten Sons of God', we can enter into the intimacy of the relationship which Jesus had with the Father, and the reason I say that is that we, too, can call him '*Abba*'. St Paul put it like this: 'You did not receive a spirit that makes you a slave again to fear, but you received the Spirit of sonship. And by him we cry, "*Abba*, Father"' (Romans 8:15).

'*Abba*' was the most intimate word for 'father'. Slaves were forbidden to address the head of the family as '*abba*'. It was the word a little child would use as it climbed on to father's lap—'daddy' would be its nearest equivalent in English. So it expresses the idea of warm intimacy and absolute trust—a relationship of dependence, true, but not of servility. We are God's beloved children, not his slaves.

There seems little doubt that '*Abba*' was the way Jesus usually addressed his Father in prayer. Some years ago the distingushed Hebrew scholar Geza Vermes made a radio programme which I produced on the Aramaic basis of the Lord's Prayer. Dr Vermes is a Jew who has written extensively on the life and ministry of Jesus—he is the author of *Jesus the Jew*. In this radio programme he tried to translate the Lord's Prayer back into the Aramaic in which it was originally spoken, and of course it began with the lovely, resonant word '*Abba*'. Somehow, hearing the prayer in that language, and begun with that word of familial love, put all the petitions in a fresh context. It is to 'Father'—even, 'Daddy'—that we come to ask that his will may be done, his kingdom come, that he will provide our daily bread and forgive our sins. It is 'Daddy' who will lead us away from temptation and deliver us from harm.

It is very poignant that in the garden of his agony, as Jesus wrestled with his human reluctance to face the horror of death on the cross, he should begin his prayer with the word '*Abba*'. The one whose will it was that this sacrifice should be made was not a remote deity demanding the fulfilment of some preordained plan, but his own loving, caring, understanding Father. Perhaps that is a lesson for us, too, when pain and testing faces us and we shrink back from it. The one whose will we seek to do is no tyrant, but '*Abba*, Father'. We are not the objects of his control, but the beloved children of his family.

▌ A reflection

God sent the Spirit of his Son into our hearts, the Spirit who calls out, 'Abba, Father.'

Galatians 4:6

A prayer

Abba, Father, help me today to trust your wise and loving will. Amen.

For discussion

How do we balance a proper reverence for God with this sense of intimate delight in our relationship with him?

Serve

'The Son of Man did not come to be served, but to serve, and to give his life as a ransom for many.'

Matthew 20:28

The kingdom of God consists of the people who serve him—who are, in the language of monarchy, his 'subjects'. Most Christians know that, believe it, even, as an article of the faith; but still find it a very difficult principle to apply in their daily lives.

The disciples of Jesus shared that difficulty. Although they heard their Master telling them that the first should be last and the last first, and 'let he who would be chief among you become servant of all', when it came to the crunch they were as anxious as we are to fight for their little bit of status. In fact, sometimes it went further than that, as when James and John came demanding a special place of privilege and honour in the coming kingdom of heaven. Yet again Jesus explained the position to them—it's not like that, that's the language of 'the Gentiles and their lords', not the language of the kingdom. In God's kingdom service is honour, the lowest place is the place of glory, the one who washes the feet is Master and Lord.

Needless to say, the message didn't register then, but it seems to have done after they had been through the trauma of Gethsemane, Calvary and the upper room. Jesus won by (apparently) losing. God's suffering servant, foretold by Isaiah, was victor over death and the grave.

So the words of Jesus in today's verse of Scripture are a profound forecast of the coming revelation of truth. Even God's

Son, the 'Son of Man', had not come into the world to be honoured or served. He neither asked nor expected to be served (waited upon). He had come to be a servant—first and foremost of God, and then of others—and to offer his life as the ransom for humankind. 'I am among you,' he told his followers, 'as one who serves.' It was the mark of his very nature—the 'Servant King', as Graham Kendrick's song calls him.

But that has enormous implications for his followers. We also are called to serve, to be servants. Indeed, we had better get used to the idea, because it will be a major occupation in heaven—'they... serve him day and night in his temple' (Revelation 7:15). And in this service there are two elements, distinguished in two different Greek words but usually translated by 'serve' in English.

The first is the idea of obedience—of the servant as, literally, slave. St Paul often called himself 'Christ's slave', and it was common in the early Church for people to think of themselves as called to be 'slaves'. They weren't implying, of course, that God or Jesus are like tyrannous slave-drivers: far from it. They were thinking of their own attitude towards their heavenly Master, and took the model of the slave, who lived only in order to do his master's bidding. That was their whole aim. This was what 'discipleship' meant for them. This word for slave (*doulos*) was used of Christian believers, of apostles, even—but not of Christ, except for that wonderful hymn to the divine humiliation in Philippians 2. There Christ is said to have taken 'the very nature of a servant' (literally, slave). Christ's servanthood was voluntary, even in this example. He laid aside his majesty. He adopted the nature of a slave, but it was for a specific purpose and for a limited time. By nature, as Philippians affirms, he was divine ('being in very nature God').

So we are Christ's slaves, gladly serving him without demanding any payment or reward. But we, like Christ, are also called to 'serve' in another way, in the sense of ministering to people's needs. It's this word (*diakoneo*) which Christ commonly applies to himself. He came to 'serve' in the sense of rendering service—washing feet, feeding the crowd, healing the sick. And he calls us, too, to 'serve' in this positive way. We are 'called to serve'—to serve others in their need, to wash feet and feed the hungry, and share in Christ's service to the world.

This 'serving' is not slavery, but perfect freedom. It has to be freely taken on, gladly accepted. Our example is the one who came 'not to be served, but to serve'. And like his, our service, too, will be costly.

A reflection

Slaves do their master's bidding. Servants meet needs.

A prayer

Lord, as you have called me to your service, make me worthy of your calling. Amen.

For discussion

In what ways can the churches we belong to 'serve' people in the name of Christ, not in order to recruit them to our cause, but simply because there is a need?

FRIDAY
Throne

'When the Son of Man comes in his glory, and all the angels with him, he will sit on his throne in heavenly glory.'

Matthew 25:31

If, like me, you enjoy visiting old churches, you may have noticed that Jesus is usually depicted either hanging on a cross or sitting on a throne. It's the second of those images that we're concerned with in this chapter.

Often, in paintings above the chancel or sanctuary, Jesus is shown sitting on his throne judging the nations. Below him is a profusion of anxious faces as they await his final verdict on their lives. To one side, and below, there is a stream of terrified people being dragged to the nether regions by devils. Sometimes the flames are licking away at the bottom of the picture. At the other side, and above, is a similar stream of people, many, it has to be said, looking quite unbearably smug, being wafted up to the bliss of heaven. The fate of both groups is clear-cut and final, and the sole arbiter of their destiny is the figure on the throne. With that facing them in church every Sunday, our medieval ancestors must have felt a powerful compulsion to do good and avoid evil!

Such notions of divine judgment are unfashionable now. But the Creed ensures that we still recognize that there is a 'judgment' and that Jesus Christ is God's appointed judge. 'He will come again in glory to judge the living and the dead, and his kingdom will have no end.' And we can't eliminate from the teaching of Jesus—right at the core of the undisputed Gospel material—his role as the final judge of the 'nations'.

There are still plenty of 'thrones' for us to see—the monarch is still enthroned in Westminster Abbey. Indeed, despite various attempts to have a less authoritarian title for the service, bishops are still 'enthroned' in their cathedrals. A 'throne' is a seat of authority, conferring on the one who sits there the right to exercise judgment. The New Testament speaks of a number of 'thrones', or places of judgment, and at times Christians have tried to distinguish the when, where and how of these various times of judgment which await different groups of people. For our purpose, however, it is sufficient to say that the throne of Christ represents the place of God's final judgment on human beings.

In the passage from which today's verse of Scripture is taken, for instance, Jesus speaks of himself as the judge of the 'nations'— *ethnoi*, in Greek... the Gentiles, the people without the Law. For them, the issue will be how they responded to the needs of 'the least of these brothers of mine'. Did they give them food, or watch them starve? Did they clothe them, or let them go naked? Did they visit them in prison, or shun them as outcasts? For myself (and following the interpretation of Oxford theologian John Fenton), I take the 'brothers of Jesus' to be his disciples, bearing the good news of the kingdom. The 'nations' will be judged by their response to them. The immediately preceding narrative in Matthew's Gospel illustrates the judgment of believers: what did we make of the gifts we were given? Believers and unbelievers alike will give an account of themselves before Christ's throne.

The picture language presents the issue in a stark, instant way, of course—like a brief hearing in a court of law. But the wider teaching of Jesus and of the Bible tells us that the judgment of God is a continuing process: we are 'being judged' all the while. Indeed, in the teaching of Jesus, if we judge ourselves rather than others, we shall not be subject to judgment (Luke 6:37). The 'judgment seat of Christ' (2 Corinthians 5:10)—a kind of tribunal rather than a throne of justice—will be the place where that process of judgment comes to its fulfilment for the Christian.

But 'God did not send his Son into the world to condemn the world, but to save the world through him.' The 'throne of judgment' is also a 'throne of grace', as the Letter to the Hebrews puts it (4:16), where our great high priest, Jesus, 'sympathises with our weaknesses' and we can find 'mercy and grace to help in time of need'.

That God's purpose is that evil will be judged there can be no doubt. But there can also be no doubt that the one who sits on the throne is the one who looks on us not with scorn, anger or hatred, but with mercy, grace and love. After all, the one who sits on the throne is the very same one who 'loved us, and gave himself for us'.

A reflection

The Judge of all is also the Saviour of all.

A prayer

Lord, help me to judge myself, to repent of what is wrong, to seek your righteousness—and to know your mercy. Amen.

For discussion

If God were simply to ignore evil and leave it unjudged, he would not be good. If he were simply to condemn human failure, he would not be love.

Righteous

'Then the righteous will shine like the sun in the kingdom of their Father.'

Matthew 13:43

In the early 1970s I was sent to a press preview of the new musical, *Godspel*—in which, we were told, the story of Jesus would be retold by a wandering band of clowns. I had no idea what to expect, and neither did most of the others in the audience. It turned out to be a remarkable experience, fresh and new and, I suppose, slightly shocking, too—after all, this was a long time ago! What struck me most about it was the way in which the story of Jesus could not only survive such a drastic piece of cultural transformation, but come across in a dynamically new way.

Early on in the show Jesus came to John to be baptized. I was familiar with the question John raised, as traditionally rendered: 'I need to be baptized by you, and do you come to me?' And I knew the answer Jesus gave: 'Let it be so now, for thus it is fitting for us to fulfil all righteousness'. Frankly, I had always understood the question, but not the answer!

In *Godspel* the answer (and I can still hear David Essex saying it) was much simpler: 'Let it be so for the present; we do well to conform in this way with all that God requires.' It was only later that I discovered that this is, in fact, the New English Bible translation.

And it conveys with particular emphasis precisely what 'righteousness' means—'conforming to all that God requires'. The 'righteous' are those who live their lives in conformity with God's requirements. Conversely, the 'unrighteous' are those who do not.

'Righteous' and 'righteousness' (in both the Hebrew and Greek versions) are among the most common words in the Bible—they occur about fifty times in the Book of Psalms alone. And they were words frequently on the lips of Jesus. 'The righteous' were those who set out to live in a way that would please God, in line with his will. And to 'hunger and thirst for righteousness' is not only to be happy—blessed—but also to be filled (fulfilled, in its true meaning). There is no higher calling. It is to be the priority of the disciple: 'Seek first God's kingdom and his righteousness.'

Sadly, the word has become corrupted. In modern English we are more likely to say 'Oh, don't be so righteous' than to approve the idea of righteousness. It's probably symptomatic of the modern way of looking at things that we're most familiar with the word in another form altogether—'self-righteous'. And that is definitely (and properly) to be condemned.

But we must not let the real meaning of 'righteous' escape. It is a lovely, positive word, speaking of one who, like Jesus himself, sets his course by God's compass and has as his chief goal doing his will. From the teaching of St Paul we know that this perfect 'righteousness' cannot be attained by human struggle, but only by the grace of God through faith. But it is still the goal. We should settle for nothing less. After all, it is the 'righteous' who will 'shine like the sun in the kingdom of their Father'.

A reflection

'Righteousness' was originally spelt in English 'rightwiseness', and that is what it is: being wise enough to do what is right.

A prayer

Lord God, deliver me from self-righteousness into the true righteousness which is your will and your gift. Amen.

PALM SUNDAY
The bread of life

'I am the bread of life.'

John 6:48

The word Jesus used in this famous saying is *artos*, which does indeed simply mean bread or a loaf. There is therefore nothing mystical or mysterious about the word itself; it described something everyone knew about, an element of everyday life of utter familiarity. But, of course, it did in fact mean much more than that. 'Bread' denoted life itself, because without it—that's to say, without food, for which it stands—we can't survive. Bread is essential to life.

In this particular passage Jesus is drawing on his hearers' knowledge of the 'manna' with which their forefathers were nourished on their journey across the desert to the Promised Land a thousand years earlier. They thought of manna as bread from heaven, which indeed it was. As Jesus said, 'My Father gave you that bread from heaven.' But the bread from heaven was ordinary food, to nourish their bodies and give them strength for their arduous journey.

Now, Jesus said, there is a new bread available to you, a bread which is not only life-sustaining but life-giving: 'If anyone eats of this bread, he will live for ever.' And where could they find this bread? 'This bread is my flesh, which I will give for the life of the world.'

Palm Sunday stands at the start of the week that changed the world. The prophet from Nazareth was welcomed to Jerusalem by his followers. As he rode his donkey down the slopes of Olivet they chanted—for all the world like a modern crowd on a cheerful 'demo'—'Come on, take over now—be king!' I realize that's not exactly what they shouted, but I think it gets very near its meaning. They wanted action from the one they now believed to be the promised Messiah. Let the Son of Man take over the kingdom. And let him do it now.

But the week would reveal that the Son of Man was working to a different agenda. He had come to bring in God's kingdom, true. But his kingly power was 'not of this world'. He had come to change things . . . indeed, to change history. But that change would begin in hearts and wills, not on the streets and in the palaces.

Actually, it began in the temple, because his kingdom was all about the rule of God. The revolution for which he called had to begin in the house of God, but it could not end there. By the end of the week the crowd would be chanting different slogans, but his challenge was still the same. 'For this cause I was born, and came into the world, to bear witness to the truth . . .'

And it is that truth revealed in Jesus that nourishes the inner needs of mankind. He is the bread of life because in him we can find all that we need for real life. The living bread—bread that gives life—is on offer now to the world. They can eat it, or reject it. What they cannot do is find another diet to meet the same need.

A reflection

'Man does not live on bread alone, but on every word that comes from the mouth of God.'

A prayer

Lord, when I am spiritually hungry, feed me with the bread that nourishes my inner life and gives me strength for the journey.

A way to pray

Self-examination: When I feel inwardly 'starved', is it because I have fed myself on the wrong bread—the bread of success, the bread of busyness, the bread of self-indulgence?

Thanksgiving: For the texture, taste and feel of bread, and for the way such an 'ordinary' thing can bring such satisfaction.

Meditation: Look at a slice of bread, or a loaf or part of a loaf. Think of all that has gone into its creation—the soil, the rain, the sun, the work of the farmer and the baker. Think of what an 'ordinary' thing bread is. And then let your mind be open to the thought that this most ordinary of things—'which earth has given and human hands have made'—can become for us the sign and seal of eternal life.

Temple

'Destroy this temple, and I will raise it again in three days.'

John 2:19

The temple dominated the religious life of Israel in the time of Jesus. Physically, it dominated Jerusalem, as anyone walking across the temple precincts today will realize. It was enormous, dwarfing everything else around it and visible on its lofty perch from many miles away. But it was equally dominant in the religious lives of the people, a place of essential and regular pilgrimage, even for Jews who lived—like the family of Jesus—at the other end of the country or in other parts of the Mediterranean world. The whole temple area was described by one Greek word (*hieron*), but the word most often used in the New Testament and by Jesus himself related to the 'sanctuary', the place that stood for the presence of God among his people. This word (*naos*) is also translated 'temple', and conveys the true and deep meaning of the temple in the life and beliefs of the Jewish people. It is the 'holy place', the sign of God's concern for and presence among the people of his covenant.

It is this 'temple', the sanctuary of God, which Jesus said his hearers could destroy and he could rebuild 'in three days'. John tells us, in one of his fascinating asides, that 'the temple he spoke of was his body'. That's a remarkable claim, because it is as good as saying that he, Jesus, could fulfil for them the same function as the sanctuary and be the sign of God's presence among his people. No wonder this claim was raised against him at his trial three years later.

'Temple' becomes a word of immense significance in the New Testament, probably arising from the way in which Jesus related to it. He was received and first honoured in the temple, by Simeon and Anna. In the temple the boy Jesus asked and answered questions of the teachers in 'his Father's house'. He drove the traders from the temple in a display of righteous anger. He taught in the temple courts. And at the moment of his death the great curtain of the temple, which divided the inner sanctuary from the outer courts, was torn in two 'from the top to the bottom'. Jesus of Nazareth, of the (non-priestly) tribe of Judah, could never enter the sanctuary of God. Jesus the Son of God, as Hebrews tells us, led the way for us into the very holy of holies, into the presence of his Father (Hebrews 10:19–22). So the earthly temple became redundant, in terms of God's purposes, replaced by a new temple, 'made without hands', the body of Christ, by which God's presence is perfectly represented among us.

More than that, as members of the 'Body of Christ', the Church, we also become a part of that temple of God. Collectively we are his 'temple': 'you yourselves are God's temple' (1 Corinthians 3:16)— that is to say, the Church represents the presence of God, his Spirit dwells among its members. But also each individual Christian is a 'temple of God'. 'Did you not know that your body is a temple of the Holy Spirit, who is in you, whom you have received from God?' (1 Corinthians 6:19).

This 'temple' metaphor is probably not one that strikes an immediate chord with modern readers, but it is more than worth reflecting on. If the Church is God's temple, and if I, as a believer, am a temple of the Holy Spirit, that has huge repercussions for the way both the Church and the believer should behave. Sin in the Church defiles God's temple. Sin in the believer conflicts with the indwelling presence of the Holy Spirit. Persisted in, I suppose, sin could destroy a church and drive away the Spirit of God from the life of the individual Christian.

In that lovely old Easter cantata 'Olivet to Calvary' there is a haunting treble solo. It is a commentary on the cleansing of the temple by Jesus, and this is its recurrent chorus: 'Another temple waits thee, Lord divine—the temple of my heart. Oh, make it thine!'

A reflection

At the heart of the temple was the holy of holies, enshrining the presence of God. What is there at the heart of the temple which is my own being and personality?

A prayer

Lord Jesus, as you cleansed the temple, with whip and scourge and words of anger, cleanse the temple of my heart of everything that offends you. Amen.

For discussion

In what ways might the Church of God need to renew and reform itself to become more truly the 'temple of God'?

TUESDAY IN HOLY WEEK

Teacher

'You call me "Teacher" and "Lord", and rightly so, for that is what I am.'

John 13:13

'Teachers' have changed in my lifetime. In my school-days, the teacher, generally speaking, stood out at the front of the class and, with all the authority that an academic gown and a university degree conveyed, 'taught' us. He or she provided the information, we received it (or not, according to preference, inclination and ability to understand). Teachers nowadays see their role very differently. They spend less time standing at the 'front' and more time moving around among the students. They are not dispensers of instant information, to be accepted and acted upon without question. They are 'enablers', who see their role as making it possible for the students to learn. In a phrase, I suppose learning is now seen as more important than teaching.

Which again, as with so many New Testament words, makes a problem for the modern reader of the Bible. When the disciples of Jesus called him 'teacher' they were putting themselves in the position of being 'disciples'—'learners'. Of course they could, and did, ask questions—one of the most common methods of learning in the world of the first century. But they saw their teacher, in this case Jesus, as the source of authoritative truth. Their questions were designed not so much to question that truth as to draw it out and apply it. The disciple typically sat at the feet of his teacher— often, literally—and drank in his words. Like the guru in Hindu and Sikh circles, he was the source of wisdom, the one to whom you turned not for an 'insight' or a 'way of seeing something', but for the truth.

It was in that sense that the disciples called Jesus 'teacher' and he accepted the title. 'Teacher' and 'Lord' more or less go together. They both speak of an authority accepted. So, when Jesus gave his disciples their final Great Commission he began it by saying that 'all authority . . . has been given to me' (Matthew 28:18). Therefore— because of that—they could go to all nations and make disciples of them . . . bring them, too, into that voluntary submission to his authority as teacher and Lord. Indeed, they were to teach them 'everything that I have commanded you'.

Normally we should instinctively reject a claim of that kind. Experience tells us that those who claim access to infallible truth are usually fantasizing. But if the one making the claim is the Son of God, the situation is radically different. The disciples drank in the words of Jesus because they recognized his uniqueness: no one taught as this man taught. And notice what the crowd said: 'He taught with authority, not like the scribes.' The scribes interpreted the teaching of others and applied it. Jesus spoke 'from God'.

It is true that Jesus made use of many of the skills and techniques of the best teachers—yes, even modern ones! He encouraged dialogue, he used story and metaphor and analogy. But the reason we make him our 'teacher' is not for his skills, but for the authority with which he spoke. With the disciples we can say, 'To whom shall we go? You have the words of eternal life.'

▍A reflection

'What gets taught is the teacher.'

▍A prayer

Divine instructor, help me to be a willing and open-minded learner as I sit at your feet. Amen.

For discussion

In what ways today can the teaching of Jesus be received? Where and how can we hear him?

Time

> **'The time has come,' he said. 'The kingdom of God is near. Repent and believe the good news!'**
>
> **Mark 1:15**

The Greeks had two words for time, *chronos* and *kairos*. The difference between them can be illustrated by eavesdropping on early-morning communication with a teenager in a typical modern household.

First, there is a loud but generally affectionate call up the stairs. 'The time (*chronos*) is seven o'clock!'

This is meant to induce a spurt of activity on the part of the drowsy scholar (who was probably listening to tapes until the early hours). In fact, of course, little happens. No feet patter to the bathroom. No taps are run.

So half an hour later a more urgent and insistent cry is to be heard. 'It's time (*kairos*) that you were getting up.'

The first kind of time refers to time on the clock or the sundial. Today it is measured by a chronometer—a measure of *chronos*. The New Testament talks of that kind of time—the second watch, the third hour of the day, things like that.

The second kind of time refers to time in the sense of destiny— 'the hour', 'the time', the moment of truth. Jesus often spoke of time in this way. 'My hour has not yet come,' he would say. Or, 'the time is coming when . . .' Or, 'the hour has come'. He saw his whole life as fulfilling a destiny, completing a work which the Father had given him to do—a work that couldn't be hurried but which would be fulfilled when the time was right. So 'the right time for me has not yet come' (John 7:6), yet it would come, and did. Sometimes this moment of destiny was *kairos* and sometimes it was *ora*, 'the hour'. In both cases, it was the pre-determined moment of truth. 'Father, the hour has come.'

The events of our salvation were not accidental, neither were they simply reactive. They were part of a greater purpose, and Jesus saw all of them as part of the great 'scheme'. God was not taken by surprise or out-manoeuvred. At the right moment, at the appointed hour, all would be revealed. So Jesus was not impatient. He trusted his heavenly Father and awaited the moment when he would be vindicated.

In modern life we are dominated by *chronos*. We run our lives, many of us, by diary and clock. We are engaged in a permanent and losing battle against time—losing, because there is never enough of it, and because time by its very nature cannot be 'defeated'. It can only be harnessed and used. It is a very wise prayer to ask, 'Lord, teach me to number my days, that I may incline my heart to wisdom.'

Perhaps we should seek rather to be committed to *kairos*, to understanding and sharing in that greater purpose of God. This is an unhurried thing, reliable and trustworthy. It is summed up in the Psalmist's words, 'I waited for the Lord.' Often what we seek from God is good and admirable and it is something he wants us to have: but not yet. The hour has not come. The *kairos* has not arrived.

There is not only a rhythm to the seasons, but a rhythm of life which is really the rhythm of God. In his time—and only in his time—all will be well.

A reflection

Time is an implacable enemy, but a good colleague.

A prayer

Lord, teach me to wait patiently for your moments in my life, not struggling to get ahead of your will and not lagging behind your purposes for me. Amen.

For discussion

What are the ways by which we can know when God's 'time' for something has arrived?

MAUNDY THURSDAY

Love

'Greater love has no-one than this, that he lay down his life for his friends.'

John 15:13

'Love' is, as the play said, a four-letter word. Actually, in the Greek of the New Testament it's several words, distinguishing brotherly love, sexual love, generosity and so on. But there is no doubt at all which love has the highest place, and it is the one described in the words of Jesus in today's verse of Scripture: *agape*, self-giving love.

This word was not exactly invented by the Christians, but they gave it a whole new meaning. For them, it was the word to describe the kind of love Jesus showed in dying for us—'Calvary love', as someone called it. It was also the kind of love Christians were to have for each other. It was love which demanded nothing in return, was unconditional and entirely free. It was a love that was expressed above all else in giving.

Sexual love (which is probably what most people mean when they use the word 'love') says, 'I love you and I want you and I'm going to have you.' *Agape* love says—as the couple do in the Marriage Service, 'All that I am I give to you, and all that I have I share with you.' The two attitudes are, frankly, poles apart. Without *agape*-love, sexual love can become selfish, demanding, even exploitative. But with it, sexual love becomes the thing of beauty and self-giving which God intended it to be.

Jesus said that the greatest love was that which involved self-sacrifice. 'Greater love has no-one than this, that he lay down his life . . .' And few of us would dispute that. Probably the real and final

133

test of love is how far we would go to demonstrate it, and it is impossible to go further than laying down our life. In his example, Jesus spoke of doing that for a 'friend'—someone for whom we have affection.

The remarkable thing about the love demonstrated in Jesus, of course, is that he went much further than that. 'God so loved the world that he gave his Son.' And the 'world' there is the same world that opposes God, society organized as though God didn't exist—the world that rejected Jesus and crucified him. God loved the *cosmos*, and gave his Son for its salvation.

St Paul puts it even more starkly: 'While we were still sinners, Christ died for us' (Romans 5:8). In this way, he argues, God 'demonstrates his own love for us': 'Very rarely will anyone die for a righteous man, though for a good man someone might possibly dare to die.' Perhaps that is comparable to laying down one's life for a 'friend'. But the love revealed in Jesus—*agape* love—goes beyond that. It sets no price and demands no returns. It does not love us because we are lovely, but because God is love.

And that is a challenge to us about the way we love others. It is not easy to love those who love us. It is harder, but not impossibly difficult, to love those we do not naturally even like. But Jesus calls his followers to love their enemies! Only true self-giving love can begin to contemplate that. Only those who understand how great the love of God is, who have looked long and hard at the figure on the cross, can begin to grasp the nature of divine love. And only in response to the love of God can we begin to learn to love with *agape* love.

▌A reflection

And now these three remain: faith, hope and love. But the greatest of these is love.

A prayer

Lord, give me a fresh understanding of your love, so that I may know in a new way what it is to love as you love. Amen.

For discussion

In everyday life, what would it mean to love our neighbours and—particularly—to love our enemies?

Peacemaker

'Blessed are the peacemakers, for they will be called sons of God.'

Matthew 5:9

I taught for five years in secondary schools. You can learn a great deal about human life in the classroom. One thing I learnt was the value of the 'peacemaker'.

Girls, especially, tend to have a 'best friend', an inseparable confidante and companion. Sometimes they were almost like Siamese twins, so that it was impossible to think of Ann without Debbie. And yet suddenly, one day, the class would assemble and they would be sitting at opposite sides of the room. Their faces told the whole story. There was a rift in the lute. The partnership was dissolved. You could feel the tension.

But there was no need to despair. For at this point Susan would come into the picture. Susan was a friend of both Ann and Debbie (but not a rival to either). During break and lunchtime she would be at work, going backwards and forwards with messages. 'She didn't mean it—she thought you'd been talking to Peter before school...' 'She wants to be friends again—if you want to...' and so on. Eventually, perhaps two days later, the class arrives in my room and once again Debbie and Ann are back together again. And in the row behind them Susan, the 'peacemaker', glows with angelic satisfaction.

'Peacemakers' make peace. I suppose that's obvious, really. But in a world of war, conflict, strife and anger, there could not be a more important role, or one closer to God's heart. Because God himself is a 'peacemaker'—he 'makes wars cease to the ends of the earth', as the Psalmist puts it. And he sent his Son Jesus to 'preach peace to those who are near, and peace to those who are far off'. The 'peacemakers' are to be sons of God because they display his likeness, reproduce his character and attributes. He is, in the words of St Paul, 'the God of peace'.

But it's worth thinking for a moment about how peace is made. Susan made peace by bringing two dissenting parties together, and she did it because she was friends with them both—she had the interests of both parties at heart. More than that, she paid the price of peace—it was her time, her effort, her patience that brought them together again. Peace always has a price, and in this case she paid it.

There is also a price for our peace, and Jesus paid that. In himself he perfectly represented both 'parties', God (because Jesus is divine) and humankind (because he is man). He set out to bring those two parties, once estranged, together again—to reconcile God and humankind. But it was no light task.

Paul, writing to the Ephesians, speaks of two parties in bitter conflict—Jews and Gentiles—being reconciled to each other and to God 'through the cross' (2:16). To the Colossians he expressed the same idea in different words: he reconciled 'all things, whether things on earth or things in heaven' to God—'by making peace through his blood, shed on the cross' (1:20). The cross of Jesus is the place of peace, because there the things that take away peace— things like anger, prejudice, greed, lust for power—can be forgiven and cleansed. That kind of peace is a victory: the victory of light over darkness. And it is a victory that brings those who were previously estranged together again.

The word 'peacemaker' was usually reserved in the ancient world for conquering emperors, who made peace by the process of destroying their enemies. And it has to be conceded that military conquest can bring about 'peace' of a sort. Jesus used it to describe a totally different kind of peace, not of conquest, but of sacrifice. The first kind of peace is temporary, until the aggrieved party is strong enough to fight again. The second kind of peace is eternal, because it actually changes people as well as situations.

A reflection

The greatest triumph isn't winning the war, but making the peace.

A prayer

Lord, make me an instrument of your peace. Where there is hatred, let me sow love. Where there is injury, pardon. For your love's sake. Amen.

For discussion

In ordinary situations of life—in the home, school, office, workshop—how can Christians in practice obey this call to be 'peacemakers'?

Remembrance

*'This is my body given for you; do this in
remembrance of me.'*

Luke 22:19

When I am visiting elderly people in the parish I notice that the
chief place of honour in the living room is usually given to a
photograph. If the person is a widow or widower, it will almost
certainly be of their husband or wife. And it stands there—very
often on the television, the focal point of the whole room—to keep
their memory alive.

That photograph is cherished. It is cleaned and its frame is well
polished. If a fire were to break out that would be the first thing to
be grabbed. It is 'only' a photograph, and the owner knows that,
but it is much more to them than simply a piece of thin card with a
grainy picture on it. It represents much happiness from the past—
holidays at the seaside, times with the children, quiet hours in the
evening together. It is a valued memorial to love and therefore in
one sense it is immortal.

In every church there is a table. Sometimes it is very ornate and
decorated, sometimes very plain and simple. And week by week
the believers in Jesus gather around it to celebrate a 'memorial' as
they share the bread and wine. 'Do this in remembrance of me,'
said Jesus—as a 'memorial', a reminder. We don't do it 'in memory
of him', like a piece of ceremonial to commemorate some great
event or person. We do it—and the word carries exactly this
meaning—to call Jesus to mind, to remind ourselves afresh what
he has done for us. Like the faded photograph, the Eucharist stirs

more than simply memories. It brings back into our consciousness joy and blessing from the past. It makes actual and 'now' what is, strictly speaking, part of history. It brings what happened long ago on Calvary into the centre of our lives now. It is in that sense that it is a 'remembrance', a calling to mind.

It is possible, I suppose, to 'do this'—that's to say, to go through the ritual of a Communion service—and fail to engage in an act of 'remembrance' at all. If that happens, then the service has lost its real meaning. It exists to stir our minds to remember, not in a passive way, but actively. Like the photo on the top of the television, it is meant to be a permanent reminder of blessing, a constant cause for thanksgiving (which is why we call it the 'Eucharist', or 'thanksgiving'). It brings him to mind.

Jesus instituted the Lord's Supper at a Passover meal. That in itself is very significant. At the Passover the Jews 'remember' the time when their forefathers were freed from slavery in Egypt. But they 'remember' the event as though it were happening now, to them—'you brought us out of the land of bondage', they say. The Passover brings the past into the present and makes it part of a living faith now.

And that is exactly what the Holy Communion is meant to do for Christians. We don't just look at the bread and wine, but consume them. They become, literally, part of us. And as we remember in this active, participative way, we are with Jesus in the upper room, we stand by the cross, we rejoice at his glorious resurrection. With all God's people—'all who stand before you in earth and heaven'— we bring an event from the past and make it part of ourselves in the present. That is what true 'remembrance' means.

▍A reflection

Remembrance makes the past real; forgetfulness wipes it out.

A prayer

Lord, create in me a deep sense of remembrance, so that what you have done in the past becomes part of my 'present'. Amen.

For discussion

Consider what, in our own lives, awakens happy memories. How do we keep those memories alive? And what might this tell us about the way that we 'remember' Jesus Christ?

The resurrection and the life

Jesus said to her, 'I am the resurrection and the life.'

John 11:25

This saying is part of a strange dialogue between Jesus and Martha, one of the sisters of Lazarus who had died four days earlier. She had chided Jesus that if he had got there earlier, her brother wouldn't have died. Jesus replied that her brother would 'rise again'.

Yes, she knew that. As a good, believing Jew of the first century, she looked for a general resurrection 'at the last day'. But excellent as that might be as a theological principle, it wasn't much comfort at that particular moment. She wanted her brother now, not at the last day.

The response of Jesus was this astonishing claim. The last day was not the resurrection. He was. 'I am the resurrection and the life.' We recite it at every funeral service and the words are as well known as almost any in the Bible. But does the enormity of his claim get to us through the mists of familiarity?

Jesus doesn't say that he can, or will, raise Lazarus from the dead (though very shortly he does). He doesn't say that at the last day he will be the agent of resurrection and the judge of the living and dead. He simply says that he is 'resurrection and life'. Within him, as part of his very being and nature, is the principle of resurrection and the principle of life. It echoes another claim he made, that as the Father has 'life in himself' so 'he has granted the Son to have life in himself', and to be the agent of life for others. 'Whoever hears my word and believes him who sent me has eternal life and will not be condemned; he has crossed over from death to life' (John 5:24–27).

This is the message of Easter—not simply that Jesus rose from the dead, but that the Son of God has authority from his Father to raise those who believe in him from death to life. When Jesus went to the cemetery to raise Lazarus from the dead, he 'called in a loud voice', 'Lazarus, come out!' Someone has suggested that if he hadn't specified who was to come out he might have emptied the graveyard. That is what Easter means to Christians: the final enemy has been destroyed.

A reflection

'I believe ... in the resurrection of the body.' So did Martha. But what Jesus asked her to do was to believe that he was the one who would bring it about. From that day, a theory or an article of the faith became part of her experience of life.

A prayer

Lord, help me today to believe with all my heart that in Jesus you have conquered death, and to thank God for that victory. Amen.

A way to pray

Self-examination: *We are all liable to fear of death—and some are 'in bondage' to it. Can I quietly and honestly face the foe today, and claim the Easter victory over it?*

Thanksgiving: *For the empty tomb of the Easter garden, and all it means.*

Meditation: *Stand, in your mind's eye, by the tomb of Lazarus and put yourself in Martha's shoes. You have heard the promise. Wait, and trust, and see it fulfilled.*